AMERICAN AUTHORS
AND CRITICS SERIES

GENERAL EDITOR

JOHN MAHONEY

University of Detroit

SHERWOOD ANDERSON AT CHATEAUGAY, NEW YORK
(*About 1916 or 1917*)

SHERWOOD ANDERSON

An Introduction and Interpretation

DAVID D. ANDERSON
Michigan State University

HOLT, RINEHART AND WINSTON, INC.

New York · Chicago · San Francisco · Toronto · London

2610459

1 2 3 4 5 6 7 8 9

For selections from *The Modern Writer* by Sherwood Anderson. Copyright 1925 by Gelber, Lilienthal Inc. Reprinted by permission of Harold Ober Associates, Inc.

For selections from *Sherwood Anderson's Memoirs* by Sherwood Anderson. Copyright 1942 by Harcourt, Brace & World, Inc. Reprinted by permission of Harold Ober Associates, Inc.

From Sherwood Anderson, "The New Note" in *The Little Review Anthology*, Margaret Anderson, editor. Copyright 1953 by Hermitage House, Inc. Reprinted by permission of Harold Ober Associates, Inc.

For quotation from Maxwell Geismar, *The Last of the Provincials*, copyright 1949 by Houghton Mifflin Company. Used by permission of Harold Ober Associates, Inc.

From Sherwood Anderson, "The American Small Town" in *The Sherwood Anderson Reader*, edited with an introduction by Paul Rosenfield. Copyright 1947 by Houghton Mifflin Company. Used with the permission of Harold Ober Associates, Inc.

For selections from *Horses and Men* by Sherwood Anderson. Copyright 1923 by B. W. Huebsch, Inc. Used by permission of Harold Ober Associates, Inc.

For a selection from *Many Marriages* by Sherwood Anderson. Copyright 1923 by B. W. Huebsch, Inc. Used by permission of Harold Ober Associates, Inc.

For selections from *Poor White* by Sherwood Anderson. Copyright 1921 by B. W. Huebsch, Inc. Used by permission of Harold Ober Associates, Inc.

For selections from *A Story Teller's Story* by Sherwood Anderson. Copyright 1924 by B. W. Huebsch, Inc. Used by permission of Harold Ober Associates, Inc.

For selections from *Triumph of the Egg* by Sherwood Anderson. Copyright 1921 by B. W. Huebsch, Inc. Used by permission of Harold Ober Associates, Inc.

For selections from *Windy McPherson's Son*, Revised Edition, by Sherwood Anderson. Copyright 1921 by B. W. Huebsch, Inc. Used by permission of Harold Ober Associates, Inc.

For selections from *Winesburg, Ohio* by Sherwood Anderson. Copyright 1919 by B. W. Huebsch, Inc., 1947 by Eleanor Copenhaver Anderson. Reprinted by permission of The Viking Press, Inc.

For selections from *Marching Men* by Sherwood Anderson. Copyright 1917 by John Lane Co. Used by permission of Harold Ober Associates, Inc.

For selections from *Mid-American Chants* by Sherwood Anderson. Copyright 1918 by John Lane Co. Used by permission of Harold Ober Associates, Inc.

For selections from *Windy McPherson's Son* by Sherwood Anderson. Copyright 1916 by John Lane Co. Used by permission of Harold Ober Associates, Inc.

For selections from *Letters of Sherwood Anderson*, edited and selected with an introduction and notes by Howard Mumford Jones in association with Walter P. Rideout. Copyright 1953 by Little, Brown & Company. Used by permission of Harold Ober Associates, Inc.

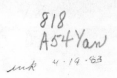
For selections from *Beyond Desire* by Sherwood Anderson. Copyright 1932 by Liveright Publishing Corporation. Used by permission of Harold Ober Associates, Inc.

For selections from *Dark Laughter* by Sherwood Anderson. Copyright 1925 by Liveright Publishing Corporation. Used by permission of Harold Ober Associates, Inc.

For selections from *Hello Towns!* by Sherwood Anderson. Copyright 1929 by Liveright Publishing Corporation. Used by permission of Harold Ober Associates, Inc.

For selections from *A New Testament* by Sherwood Anderson. Copyright 1927 by Liveright Publishing Corporation. Used by permission of Harold Ober Associates, Inc.

From *Tar: A Midwest Childhood* by Sherwood Anderson. Copyright 1926 by Liveright Publishing Corporation. Used by permission of Harold Ober Associates, Inc.

From *Sherwood Anderson's Notebook* by Sherwood Anderson. Copyright 1926 by Liveright Publishing Corporation. Used by permission of Harold Ober Associates, Inc.

For quotations from *The Chicago Renaissance in American Letters* by Bernard Duffey. Copyright 1954 by Michigan State College Press.

For four illustrations from the Sherwood Anderson collection. Reproduced by permission of The Newberry Library.

For selections from *Puzzled America* by Sherwood Anderson. Copyright 1935 by Charles Scribner's Sons. Used by permission of Harold Ober Associates.

For quotations from Sherwood Anderson, "Grass Root News," and a letter in *Sherwood Anderson, His Life and Works* by James Schevill. Copyright 1951 by University of Denver Press; used by permission of the publisher, University of Denver Press.

For quotations from *Nearer the Grass Roots* by Sherwood Anderson. Copyright 1929 by The Westgate Press. Used by permission of Harold Ober Associates.

Acknowledgment is also made to Mrs. Sherwood Anderson for her invaluable assistance and kind generosity.

ABOUT THE AUTHOR: DAVID D. ANDERSON, former Fulbright Lecturer at the University of Karachi, Pakistan, teaches American Thought and Language at Michigan State University. He is the author of *Louis Bromfield, Critical Studies in American Literature* and numerous articles and short stories. He received the M.S.U. Book Manuscript Award for the manuscript of *Sherwood Anderson.*

*Once more,
to Pat*

PREFACE

Sherwood Anderson, an acknowledged master of the short-story form and a major influence on the evolutionary course of modern prose fiction, is one of the most widely anthologized and analyzed of twentieth-century American authors. At the same time the respect given his work is often grudging, many of his works are ignored, and others are frequently distorted to fit critical preconceptions. Therefore, the purpose of this volume is to clarify the uncertain and ambiguous place that Anderson holds in American letters and to attempt to point out the direction that a critical evaluation of Anderson's work must take if his works are to be assessed properly.

Consequently, I believe that in order to understand Anderson's works in their proper relationship to his complexity of purpose, all his works must be approached as a chronological unit—viewed in the realm outside the space-time continuum. The modern critic must employ all his faculties of perception in order to assess both artistic meaning and accomplishment. No critic has yet examined in detail the close relationship between Anderson's life and his work, and I am convinced that such an examination is vital to understanding his work and determining his contribution to American literature.

This book, then, is a critical biography. It is not definitive, but it introduces new critical concepts: that Anderson's work did not deteriorate seriously in his later years, but instead took new directions; that Anderson's writing techniques are firmly rooted in American literary traditions; that Anderson is part of the mainstream of American romantic idealism; that Anderson's work can properly be understood only in the context in which it was written.

My goals are understanding, definition, and appreciation of a unique literary canon; if this book makes any contribution, however small, to reaching these goals, I shall be satisfied.

Lansing, Michigan   D. D. A.
December 1966

CONTENTS

ILLUSTRATIONS

CHRONOLOGY

1876	Sherwood Anderson born September 13, in Camden, Preble County, Ohio, to Irwin and Emma Anderson.
1884	Family settled in Clyde, Ohio after living in several Ohio towns.
1884–1896	Attended public school and worked at a variety of jobs, from newsboy to stable hand. Acquired the nickname "Jobby."
1895	Enlisted in Company I, 16th Infantry, Ohio National Guard. Emma Anderson, Sherwood's mother, died.
1896	Moved to Chicago in the fall and worked in an apple warehouse.
1898–1899	Served in Company I, Sixth Ohio Regiment of Volunteer Infantry in the South and on Cuban occupation duty. Discharged as corporal.
1899–1900	Worked on a farm near Clyde and attended Wittenburg Academy, Springfield, Ohio. Graduated in June 1900 and took an advertising job in Chicago.
1900–1906	Sold advertising space and wrote advertising copy.
1904	Married Cornelia Lane on May 16, in Toledo, Ohio. Settled in Chicago.
1906	Moved to Cleveland in the fall to become president of United Factories Company.
1907	First son Robert, born on August 16. Moved to Elyria, Ohio as "the roof-fix man," president of a mail-order paint company, later the Anderson Manufacturing Company.
1908	Second son John, born on December 31.
1911	Daughter Marion, born on October 29.
1912	Found dazed in Cleveland on December 1. Hospitalized briefly for nervous exhaustion.
1913	Left Elyria in February. Returned to Chicago and worked for advertising company.
1913–1921	Associated with the Chicago literary renaissance. Wrote and sold advertising. Continued serious writing.
1914	"The Rabbit-Pen," first short story, published in *Harper's* (July).
1915–1916	Divorced Cornelia Lane in fall of 1915. Married Tennessee Mitchell in 1916. *Windy McPherson's Son*, first novel, published.
1917	*Marching Men* published.
1918	*Mid-American Chants* published.
1919	*Winesburg, Ohio* published.

1920	Irwin Anderson, Sherwood's father, died. Spent the winter in Mobile, Alabama, recuperating from influenza.
1921	*Poor White* published. Spent three months in Europe, met Gertrude Stein. Won *Dial* prize in October. *Triumph of the Egg* published in fall.
1922	Left Chicago and advertising permanently; broke with Tennessee. Went to New York, met Elizabeth Prall.
1923	*Many Marriages* published. Went to Reno in February to establish residency for divorce. *Horses and Men* published in fall.
1924	Divorced Tennessee Mitchell in January. Married Elizabeth Prall. *A Story Teller's Story* published. Moved to New Orleans.
1925	Went on lecture tour in January–February. *Dark Laughter* and *The Modern Writer* published. Wandered through the South; purchased Ripshin Farm, Troutdale, Virginia.
1926	*Tar: A Midwest Childhood* and *Sherwood Anderson's Notebook* published.
1927	*A New Testament* published. Bought the two weekly newspapers of Marion, Virginia; edited and published them.
1928	Began wandering again.
1929	*Hello Towns!* published in the fall; *Nearer the Grass Roots* and *Alice and the Lost Novel* published in limited editions. Separated from Elizabeth Prall and continued wandering.
1930	Met Eleanor Copenhaver. Visited mill towns with her and supported workers and strikers in their struggles with mill owners.
1931	*Perhaps Women* published. Went on lecture tour in the fall. Was attracted to Communism.
1932	Divorced Elizabeth Prall. Spent much time in Marion; lectured; supported "Bonus Army." Attended "World's Congress against War" in Amsterdam, August–September. *Beyond Desire* published.
1933	Married Eleanor Copenhaver in July. *Death in the Woods* published. Supported New Deal.
1934	Traveled for Today and wrote articles on his observations. *No Swank* published in limited edition. Worked on stage version of *Winesburg, Ohio.*
1935	*Puzzled America* published.
1936	*Kit Brandon* published.
1937	*Plays: Winesburg and Others* published.
1938	Worked at unfinished novels; started the *Memoirs.*
1939	Wrote *Home Town.* Lectured at writers' conferences; *A Writer's Concept of Realism,* lecture given at Olivet College, Michigan, published.
1940	*Home Town* published. Worked on the *Memoirs.*
1941	Died March 8 at Colon, Panama Canal Zone, of peritonitis.
1942	*Sherwood Anderson's Memoirs* published in March.

INTRODUCTION

For more than 30 years it has been stylish for critics to regard Sherwood Anderson's *Winesburg, Ohio* and a handful of his individual short stories as solid literary achievements and to dismiss the bulk of his work (often apparently unread by the critics) as failures, or, more charitably, as not quite satisfying. Such criticism of Anderson's work tends to take either one of two directions: the first is an attempt to combine subjective value judgments and sweeping generalities in brief essays that purport to give the modern reader, in a few dozen pages, all he needs to know about the works. The second attempts to be comprehensive and thus fair to all or most of Anderson's work. Ultimately, however, this approach becomes bogged down in biography and Freudian analysis, both of which are fascinating byways, but neither is an adequate substitute for careful examination of the works themselves.

Both of these critical approaches are for obvious reasons unsatisfactory. The first variety, while often well written, says little about Anderson's most famous works and nothing about the lesser known, and depends for its effect upon the condescending pity of its conclusions. The second, while attempting to unravel the web of biography, autobiography, myth, and fabrication surrounding Anderson's writing, bogs down in side issues and results in critical biographies that turn out to be unsatisfactory as either criticism or biography.

Criticism, in order to interpret a writer's meaning and to determine the relative success or failure of the techniques he employs, as well as to establish the relation of the writer's individual works to his work as a whole, must be firmly based on careful textual examination. In the case of Sherwood Anderson, this method has not been used consistently by any critic. (Maxwell Geismar in his criticism of Anderson in *The Last of the Provincials* comes close to employing this approach, but the essay is too brief to examine all the works in necessary detail.)

Critics have made much of the fact that the bulk of Anderson's work is autobiographical. He has been identified with the protagonists of most of his novels and a good many of his short stories; in addition, he wrote three volumes of autobiographical sketches and memoirs, as well as six of essays, one of journalistic writings, and the text of a photographic essay. Such a concentration on oneself is dangerous from a critical point of view, because it gives rise to complaints that the writer lacked objectivity and the ability to select artistically, and that he did not grow intellectually. All these criticisms have been directed at Anderson by those who complain that he was so fascinated with the wonder of his escape from the world of industrialism to that of the writer that he was unable to grow into the literary gianthood that had been prophesied for him early in his career.

Such criticism does have some justification, but it does not tell the whole truth about either the man or his work, and to accept it as such is unjust. Anderson's works were essentially autobiographical, as he frequently admitted in his letters and published memoirs, but, as he further pointed out, his autobiographical writing was not intended to focus on facts but on feelings—not on names, dates, and places, but on meanings. As a result it is evident that his works as a whole comprise a multivolume spiritual autobiography that records and analyzes the impressions of generic man during the unique period that saw America transformed from an agricultural to an industrial state.

This change in the American scene took place during Anderson's own lifetime, and it was felt most suddenly and spectacularly in his own Midwest. His works attempt to analyze and interpret that experience, ranging from Tar's initial awareness of the mystery of life in *Tar: A Midwest Childhood* through man's attempt to regain his individuality in *Many Marriages*; and through the initial impact of industrialism in *Poor White* and the inarticulate attempts of the worker to cope with the machine in *Marching Men* into ultimate contamination of the countryside and the individual in *Beyond Desire*. That Anderson's own experiences play a central role in these works is obvious, but the material facts have been transmuted into an analytical biography of an era.

It is apparent not only that Anderson devoted his works to a careful analysis of the time in which he lived, but also that he was continually coming closer to recognizing the implications of that period. Through what seems to be repetition, but what actually proves to be closer and more careful examination of the material with which life provided him, Anderson came to some conclusions that may be the only possible ones that can shed light on the meaning of our time.

It is my argument that Anderson's works, in all their variety of forms, from short story to essay to novel to autobiographical memoir, must be approached as a unit; that the works as a whole provide the record of one man's attempt to understand the relation between the individual and the time in which he lived and to determine the ultimate meaning of that relation.

In any attempt to establish the validity of such a thesis, several factors must be taken into consideration. First, the works must be examined chronologically in order to determine what Anderson learned about the relation between the individual and the era. Second, this examination must focus on the works themselves. Because Anderson's own life, as well as his letters, often aid interpretation, they must be discussed where necessary, but only insofar as they lend to an understanding of the works. Third, all of Anderson's published works and many of his unpublished ones must be examined.

For purposes of convenience the works may be divided into three major periods: 1916–1918, when Anderson first began to analyze the American scene; 1919–1929, the period during which his analysis became close and penetrating; and 1929–1939, when he began to formulate conclusions.

1

ORIGIN OF THE ANDERSON MYTH

ON March 9, 1941, the Elyria, Ohio, *Chronicle-Telegram* carried a news article headed "Sherwood Anderson, Former Elyria Manufacturer, Dies." Could Anderson have read it, he would have been amused by its irony, because the death of Anderson the industrialist had taken place almost thirty years before, when Sherwood Anderson, writer and determined literary artist, was born.

When Elyria knew Anderson, he was living proof of the myth propagated by Horatio Alger. From a poor boyhood he had risen to respectability and the threshold of wealth, and he was a disciple of the new materialism. To all this, Elyria gave its approval. But this was before February 1913, when Anderson made his final break with industrialism, with Elyria, and with the standards and values of both. Anderson himself did not understand the break, as shown in the essay "When I Left Business for Literature" and in the equally vague explanation in *A Story Teller's Story*, but the nature of Anderson's formative years made such a breach inevitable.[1]

Sherwood Anderson was born in Camden, Preble County, Ohio, on September 13, 1876, just as the gilded age of American materialism was getting under way. Irwin Anderson, his father, was an Ohio Civil War cavalryman and a skilled and prosperous harness maker; Emma Smith Anderson, his mother, was a former serving girl, who married his father when she was twenty. His father and his mother play important roles in many of Anderson's later works as he attempted to understand them, and his varying interpretations of them make it difficult to determine now how much of their factual backgrounds he actually knew. However, there is often a great deal of

[1] Many of the facts of Anderson's early life discussed in this chapter have been taken from the unpublished doctoral dissertation by William Sutton, *Sherwood Anderson: The Formative Years (1876–1913)*, The Ohio State University, 1943.

difference between the facts of their lives and Anderson's portrayals of them.

Irwin Anderson was not the southern dandy that Anderson described in his writing, but the son of a prosperous, hard-working farmer who had pioneered in Ohio. After a brief postwar excursion to the South, the elder Anderson had settled down to practice his trade in rural Ohio. He was popular, played in the town band, and taught in the Sunday School; above all, he was a storyteller in the rural Midwestern oral tradition. Sherwood was the third child after Karl, the artist, and his only sister, Stella.

At about the time of Sherwood's birth Irwin's luck started to change, and the rest of his life was influenced by forces that he did not understand and that Sherwood, only after years of trying, finally did comprehend as he came to know and to identify himself with his father. As machine-made harnesses began to compete with the handcrafted variety, Irwin's business fell off, and he increasingly took refuge in storytelling and drinking. When his shop failed, he began a series of moves to other Ohio towns, attempting to practice his trade in an economic atmosphere that had less and less room for it. In Caledonia his life touched briefly with Warren G. Harding's, but Harding, on the crest of the times, moved to Marion and eventually to the White House; the Andersons moved on to Clyde and into obscurity.

Clyde was the only town Sherwood remembered, and there the family fortunes declined rapidly. Unable to open a shop, Irwin worked for others, first in a harness shop, and later in small factories and as a painter. He drank more and more and sought his only satisfaction in storytelling among his cronies while his wife struggled to maintain the family, now augmented by three younger sons—Earl, Ray, and Irving. This was the family image that Sherwood grew up with, and for many years he accepted the view of Irwin Anderson that Clyde saw: humorous, likable, but not of much account. He later learned to despise his father. He loved his mother, who died worn out in 1895, although she was always to remain an enigma to him.

The Anderson family's hold on respectability was precarious through the 1880s and early 1890s. Irwin changed jobs as other men change moods; Sherwood's sister, Stella, helped support the family by teaching school, and as soon as they were old enough to work, the boys did odd jobs, selling newspapers and helping their father paint signs and barns. But the family was not desperately poor; in nineteenth-century America children were expected to help out when they became old enough.

These years in Clyde were extremely important in forming the two lives of Sherwood Anderson. He perceived very early that his family was not like the families of many of his friends, and in his early teens he found out why. Many of the people of Clyde, like most Americans in the late nineteenth century, were imbued with the spirit of the age. America was growing, expanding, booming, and providing opportunities to join forces with industrialism and commerce and to grow along with the country. Many of Clyde's people did so, but Irwin Anderson could not; and this spirit, more than a reaction against Irwin's ways, probably accounts for Sherwood's ambition. He became known as "Jobby" Anderson, a bright, alert boy who was willing to work hard at anything at which he could make money. Sherwood, like his fictional counterpart in *Tar: A Midwest Childhood,* hustled at every job he could find, eager to work his way up.

At the same time, something else was in the air in Clyde, a spirit that was less obvious to the ambitious boy than the atmosphere of materialism, but that became increasingly important to him as he became a man and a writer. This was the fact that Clyde was a reservoir of nineteenth-century Midwestern traditions. Unconsciously, through the stories of his father, the talk at the local race track, and his everyday contacts and activities, Sherwood absorbed the sense of closeness to others and to nature, of neighborliness, of an awareness of life in the growing things of the countryside. Above all, he became aware of people and of the bittersweetness of their lives. Clyde had an air of intimacy and of friendly concern that Sherwood was to remember and to seek again as he grew older.

In Clyde, Anderson grew from childhood to young manhood. He was not only a hustler, but, like Tom Sawyer, he was a pirate, an adventurer, an idler in summer sunshine; he too had his cave, which can still be seen near his old home. His ambition developed and he performed well but not brilliantly as a student, quitting high school to work in the local bicycle factory. At 19 he enlisted in the local National Guard company.

At this time, his intimate world began to disintegrate. His mother died, officially of tuberculosis, and his father could not keep the

SHERWOOD "JOBBY" ANDERSON (ABOUT 1888)

7

family together. Karl, ambitious to paint, left for Chicago shortly after, and Sherwood, after working as a stable groom for a year, followed in the fall of 1896. Convinced that there, through hard work, he could become wealthy and powerful, Sherwood joined the influx of country boys depicted by Carl Sandburg, as they poured into Chicago in the late nineteenth century.

The Clyde *Enterprise* reported that he had a "lucrative position" in the big city, and indeed he had—rolling barrels of apples in a warehouse. At night he roamed the city, alternately awed and repulsed by what he saw. Nevertheless, when the Spanish-American War threatened, he wrote that he was eager and ready to go. The *Enterprise* commented favorably on his spirit, and although he later deprecated his enthusiasm and commented that war service was better than rolling barrels in a warehouse, there is nevertheless no reason to question his eagerness. Manifest destiny was part of the America he was seeking, and he was very much a child of the times. It was only later that many sensitive Americans like Anderson came to regard that war as ludicrous if not dishonorable.

Anderson's war service was short and comparatively uneventful. After a patriotic send-off the Clyde company became Company I, Sixth Ohio Regiment of Volunteer Infantry. It trained at Chickamauga, Georgia, and Camp Poland, Tennessee, and then, after the brief war was over, served on occupation duty in Cuba for four months. Company I was given a lavish welcome home in May 1899, and Anderson was mustered out as a corporal. He thoroughly enjoyed his war experience.

The war period had provided important personal experiences for him. He was fascinated by an almost mystic concept of the unity inherent in large bodies of men working and marching together, welded into a nonthinking but strong-feeling mass. This concept became the basis for *Marching Men*, and it accounted for much of his continued preoccupation with the power of men and machines in factories.

Although he was influenced by this concept of physical force into the 1930s, Anderson saw its dangers. While he knew that men become united through mass action, he was also aware that they lose individuality in the process and that often they are bruised and battered by mass activity. Anderson observed this effect in the training camps, and it perhaps accounts for his inability to conclude *Marching Men* decisively, for his lifelong unwillingness to identify himself completely with any mass movement, and for his distrust of communism.

The army, however, provided Anderson with another important experience. He saw his company as a microcosm of late nineteenth-century America. The company street was Main Street, and in a town of tents all barriers were down. Anderson lived intimately with all the men, from the banker's son to the ne'er-do-well. Men showed themselves as they were in a way that social, religious, and economic barriers made impossible in Clyde.

Having traveled, served his country, and seen something of the world, Anderson returned briefly to Clyde. He rejected the idea of returning to the apple warehouse, where his brother Irving was working, and went on to Springfield, Ohio, where Karl, Stella, and Earl were living. Karl was drawing illustrations for *The Woman's Home Companion,* and Stella was teaching. After living with Karl for a while, Sherwood returned to Clyde, worked on a farm for the summer, and then in the fall returned to Springfield, again moving in with Karl. He planned to complete high school at the Wittenberg Academy in order to enter Wittenberg College. At 23, a grown man and a veteran, he worked diligently, both in school and as a handyman. He graduated from the academy on June 4, 1900, and gave a commencement address on Zionism.

In later years Anderson ignored this phase of his career, mentioning briefly in his *Memoirs* only that he had attended the college rather than the academy. However, he was attracted by both the world of business and the world of ideas as he came in close contact with them in Springfield. Trilena White, a schoolteacher, introduced him to books, and Harry Simmons, advertising manager of Crowell Publishing Company, gave him a job selling advertising in the firm's Chicago office. Stella, Irving, Ray, and probably Earl had gone to Chicago by that time, and he joined them. The sense of family was still strong in him at 24, as it was to be for the rest of his life.

At the time Anderson joined Crowell as an advertising salesman, the advertising man was a booster who could tell a story, hustle an account, and take advantage of a break. Anderson was good at all three. At first his job was insecure; the Chicago manager of the Crowell firm had wanted to hire someone else. Then a manufacturer ordered two hundred lines of copy, and when Anderson was sent to arrange for the signing of the contract, he learned the order was a mistake and that the manufacturer had wanted two thousand lines. After telegraphing his company that he had engineered the increase, Anderson returned to Chicago to a raise in salary and a secure place for himself in the Crowell advertising department.

He soon learned that he could handle words, and he began to write copy. He moved to the Frank White agency as a copywriter, and after its merger with Long-Critchfield, he stayed on, traveling and soliciting accounts, for which he wrote the copy. In his mid-20s Anderson was well on his way to success, and he began to act and dress the part of a rising young businessman.

During this time he wrote numerous articles for advertising trade journals. In 1903 he wrote a column called "Rot and Reason" in *Agricultural Advertising,* and in 1904 he wrote one called "Business Types" in *The Reader.* In both, the philosophy of the booster predominates, and in "Push, Push, Push" the eager ambition of young "Jobby" Anderson is made articulate. There is nothing of the tongue-in-cheek quality in these writings; the sincerity displayed in them is unquestionable. In "The Born Quitter," however, he injected a sly plea for the unsuccessful, and in another article he frankly admitted that the only goal of business is making money. He remembered later that his only interests at the time were in boosting and in showing off his success.

Still, however, changes were taking place in his thinking. In *Memoirs* he testifies that he had begun to cheat a bit; while on trips he wrote his copy hurriedly and then took time to walk the streets of little towns, "thinking." He submitted a story to the *Saturday Evening Post* at the request of its editor, George H. Lorimer, whose attention had been called to Anderson by Cyrus Curtis, a reader of *Agricultural Advertising.* The story was rejected, however, because it did not glorify business and the businessman— yet at about the same time Anderson gave a speech on "making good." Clearly his faith in the American myth was no longer entirely unshaken.

Meanwhile Anderson had begun to court his future wife. On one of his advertising trips he met Cornelia Lane, the daughter of a prosperous Toledo, Ohio, shoe wholesaler and deacon in the First Baptist Church of Toledo. She was a graduate of Western Reserve University, a sorority girl, a literary editor of the school annual, and a devotee of the University Theatre. After her graduation she traveled in Europe. Cornelia Lane represented, in fact, all the things that Anderson was not and was painfully aware that he was not. She was attractive, well educated, refined; he was self-assured, had

THE ANDERSON BROTHERS AND SISTER
left to right: KARL, RAY, SHERWOOD, STELLA, IRVING, EARL (PHOTOGRAPH TAKEN
ABOUT 1900)

11

a way with words, and dressed like a dandy, with overtones of the race track and the smoking car. Perhaps their mutual attraction resulted from these contrasts. It would be pleasant to assume that they shared literary interests, but Anderson was largely untutored and unread. They were married on May 16, 1904, and after a brief honeymoon settled in a Chicago apartment.

Anderson was always reluctant to speak of the years of this first marriage, and Cornelia has chosen to remain silent, but it is evident that during the next few years, under Cornelia's tutelage, the direction of Anderson's life changed drastically. Not only did she introduce him to the social graces, but more significantly they spent many evenings together reading aloud. From Cornelia, Anderson learned of the existence of that elusive quality called taste, and he learned, too, that words could be combined in ways that were esthetically pleasing as well as functional.

In the fall of 1906 Anderson left Chicago to become president of the United Factories Company, a Cleveland firm that specialized in direct mail advertising and selling for companies that subscribed to its service. The change was an opportunity for Anderson to move up to a position where he could match titles, if not salary, with his father-in-law and escape the vague dissatisfaction he felt with the advertising business. Nevertheless, his duties were much the same; he wrote brochures and copy and traveled to solicit new business for the firm.

Evidence of his new understanding of the power of words is found in one of the brochures: "If you are not satisfied," he wrote, "you can feel free about taking the matter up with me personally, and I promise you that I will not . . . pile up words to confuse you. . . ." At the same time, he tried to place the business on the same person-to-person basis that he had known along Main Street in Clyde.

Anderson tried to be a good company president and a good family man. At home Cornelia introduced poetry and French lessons. But the business was a fiasco. Trouble resulted from his sale of defective incubators, and Anderson struggled to salvage his personal integrity and the financial stability of his firm. He maintained his integrity, but emerged disillusioned. Meantime, on August 16, 1907, a son, Robert, had been born.

Anderson now realized that he was in a trap and that he must escape. He felt that the new age conspired against honesty, to which he was fully committed. In attempting to find a compromise, in late 1907 he started a mail order paint business in nearby Elyria. Here, in a quieter, less grasping way of life, he felt that the good life might yet be attained. But Elyria, like Clyde, was infected with the virus of materialism, and Anderson knew that he had to produce. He joined the Elks and the country club; he dreamed of expensive colleges for his children; and he became "the roof-fix man," president of the Anderson Manufacturing Company, which began manufacturing its own paint in 1908. The venture was a success from the start.

Essentially Anderson was concerned with sales promotion and advertising. Again he attempted to conduct the business on a personal note, but a bit of cynicism crept into the brochures, one of which, showing the back of a man's head, was captioned "This is the Roof of the Roof-Fix Man." Shortly after this he started a scheme which he termed "commercial democracy," a plan to sell shares of stock to paint dealers. In a little magazine of the same name he advocated a close personal relation between manufacturer and dealer and hinted vaguely at a new socialistic economic order that the plan, if successful, would bring about.

It is doubtful if the Elyria business and professional men who subscribed to stock in the resulting company, the American Merchants Company, knew that Anderson was planning such economic heresy. Rather, it must have seemed like a good venture, for the company was capitalized at $200,000, of which Anderson held $25,000 in stock, and he was in complete charge. Evidently he still planned to succeed, but it was a different sort of success from that he had anticipated only a few years before in Chicago. Not only had its scope narrowed considerably, but his reaction against the conventional kind of commercial success was becoming pronounced.

Meanwhile Anderson's family life was apparently happy. Two more children had been born, John in 1908 and Marion in 1911. With other businessmen of the town Anderson belonged to service and social organizations; Cornelia was active in the Fortnightly Literary Club; and both belonged to a discussion club. From all indications Anderson's home life, like his business life, was secure and promising, and the family was destined to find a solid place for itself in Elyria.

Surface appearances were deceiving, however, and the growing disenchantment evidenced in his advertising work was symptomatic of even more serious doubts which Anderson was keeping to himself. Several Elyria residents began to think him moody, a bit radical, and increasingly careless about his appearance. In *Memoirs* he noted that he was suddenly struck with the meaninglessness of what he was doing, and he later stated that it was in Elyria in 1911 that he began to drink, chase women, and then write. Essentially his writing was undirected, at least at first. He recalled, "I quit wanting to change people. I began to want more and more to understand rather than change," thus starting almost at once the course that his writing was to take throughout his life, in a career that was devoted not to changing but to understanding.

His writing was not the secret sin that he pictured in *A Story Teller's Story,* but, rather, almost common knowledge, perhaps even an exciting idea to the people in their small literary circles. As Anderson recalled, probably with accuracy, Cornelia was not hostile to it—she was merely skeptical; and Anderson, conscious of the educational gap between them, resented her attitude. Neither discouraging nor encouraging his writing, she was planting the seeds of self-doubt that were to plague him for years. Her efforts to help him with grammar, punctuation, and spelling were humbly accepted, but their relationship became strained, and time that Anderson should have devoted to business was spent writing. He often mentioned that in Elyria he had written and then destroyed the manuscript for a book called *Why I Am a Socialist,* but none of his Elyria acquaintances ever remembered having seen it. If the book actually was written, Anderson was still too shrewd in the game of business ever to let it get out of his hands. Yet he continued to write.

During these years of uncertainty, depression, and frustration, the origins of the Anderson myth began to take form, rising partially from the fact that Anderson himself was unable to discuss the period with any degree of objectivity until many years later when he wrote *Memoirs,* published after his death. Even then, years later, however, he was unable to force himself to be complete and impersonal; yet he revealed that much of his anguish of the time stemmed from the quandary he was in. On the one hand he felt an obligation to his family, and on the other he was unable to go on with what he was doing. Perhaps the shadow of Irwin Anderson's improvidence haunted him. It was a situation in which he could not do the right thing, and even in later years he was unable to acknowledge that he could not or would not discharge his family obligations. The specter of family haunted him almost always, until years later when he gathered his children around him in Virginia.

Anderson forced himself to forget many facts, among them the details of his writing that his associates remembered. His secretary recalled typing several stories during 1911 and 1912, which were sent off to publishers and subsequently rejected. More important, friends remembered that both *Windy McPherson's Son* and *Marching Men* were conceived, and the first drafts written, in Elyria; stockholders in his company remembered him writing at his desk when he should have been tending to business. Whether it was a substitute for drink, as he later recalled, or not, clearly the image of success that "Jobby" Anderson knew had become something he was desperately trying to understand. As the later published versions of the novels indicate, he had completed his rejection of materialistic values, but he had no idea of what was next.

The quandary he was caught in was not easy to solve. In his business life he found it impossible to put into practice the human values he had derived from Clyde and from his experiences in the army; his efforts to determine, through his writing, what had gone wrong in American life were not only ineffectual but scorned; and he had a position and a family to maintain, neither of which was responsible for his present predicament. Such a condition could not last indefinitely, and in late November 1912 the event occurred that gave rise to the Anderson myth—that he suddenly rejected business and materialistic values in order to devote his life to writing. The myth has been perpetuated by Anderson and his friends, in spite of the fact that it contains only the spirit, not the essence, of truth.

As Anderson later described the incident, his departure from the Anderson Manufacturing Company was abrupt, conscious, and yet mystical. Suddenly, in the midst of dictating a letter to his secretary, he stopped, at once overwhelmed by the sordidness of his business career. He toyed with the idea of giving a rational explanation for his sudden decision to quit, and then decided against it. In a moment that he said was dominated either by shrewdness or by insanity, he looked at his feet and said, "I have been wading in a long river and my feet are wet." After a moment he continued, "My feet are

cold, wet, and heavy from long walking in a river. Now I shall go
walk on dry land." [2] With that, he walked out the door and along
the railroad tracks, determined to devote the rest of his life to
literature.

Such an explanation overlooks Anderson's mental state at the
time, his innate sense of responsibility and practicality, and the
accounts of the episode that appeared in Elyria and Cleveland newspapers. The evidence points either to an ill-conceived attempt to run
away or to a temporary mental breakdown; it tends to support the
latter view. The facts of his actual leaving have never been established, but on December 2, 1912, the Elyria *Evening Telegram*
carried a news story headed "Elyria Man Is Found Dazed in Cleveland." The story states that Anderson was found dazed and in-
coherent in Cleveland and was hospitalized, suffering from nervous
exhaustion. His condition was ascribed to overwork; the article
concluded:

> Added to the cares of the Anderson Manufacturing Co. and other
> enterprises in which Anderson was the guiding spirit, for the last
> several months he has been working on a novel and at odd times
> has been writing stories for magazines. Engrossed in writing Anderson
> worked many a night until nearly dawn and then attended to
> business affairs.
> Two months ago he was warned by a physician that he was over-
> working and . . . friends . . . only a week ago remarked his
> fagged out condition.

This report, corroborated by articles in the Cleveland *Press* and
the Cleveland *Leader,* disputes his own fanciful accounts in the
Century and in *A Story Teller's Story* and the even more incorrect
version in the *Memoirs*. In each of those versions Anderson implied
that he never returned to Elyria and that his business and family
were left stranded. Although he did return to both, it was nevertheless this incident that made his break mandatory.

A few days later the Elyria paper carried a final account headed
"Sherwood Anderson Will Write Book on Experiences as Nomad."
The article stated that Anderson had "through deep thought" deliberately thrown himself into a trance for the experience in order
that he might understand it. Perhaps he believed this himself, but

---

[2] Sherwood Anderson, "When I Left Business for Literature," *Century,* cvii
(August, 1924), 494.

the earlier news story suggests another explanation. This fantastic account seems to be another manifestation of Anderson's lifelong need to explain and to justify his actions in his fiction, his auto-biographies, his letters, and in the series of prefaces, forewords, and notes with which he introduced his works. There was much skepticism in Elyria about whether or not Anderson was really sick at the time—in all probability he was. His mind was demanding that he find a way out of the quandary he had put himself in.

After a brief hospitalization and a short vacation in Toledo, Anderson returned to Elyria. He had made up his mind to dispose of the business, either because he was determined to find a job that would allow him to devote more time to writing or because the Andersons felt that after such an episode they could no longer stay in Elyria. Probably both factors were responsible, for he began to wind up his business affairs on his return, and the Elyria *Democrat* carried a notice in its February 16, 1913, issue that Anderson had decided to return to Chicago to the Taylor-Critchfield Advertising Company. Three days later he left, to be followed by Cornelia and the children when he had made preparations for them.

The break that Anderson made with business was not at this point a physical one, as he would have us believe, but a very definite spiritual break. Although he was to continue writing advertising copy, much of it in the same boosting vein, for another ten years, he no longer believed what he wrote. Rather, he reserved his belief for the personal writing that had become more and more important to him, especially after he became imbued with the esthetic atmosphere of the Chicago renaissance. The important fact was that his ideological ties were broken, that he knew the American dream had become corrupted, and that he believed that if he examined that dream as he had known it, he would come to understand it and perhaps to find a solution to the inevitable dehumanization which accompanied its failure. The Elyria years that had provided him with the most promise for material success were behind him, deliberately rejected because for him the standards they represented proved to be meaningless, and his life took a new direction.

Almost 37, with a trunk full of manuscripts, Anderson was taking a decisive step, but not one that would destroy him if he failed. He could always write copy, just as he planned to do in the immediate future, whether he believed it or not. Without knowing it, however, he was taking the only step that could make his writing come alive. The heady atmosphere of Chicago in its most fertile literary period would provide the needed impetus, together with much dross that he would have to learn to reject. If he had deliberately foreseen what was ahead, he could not have made a more opportune decision to combine ambition, a way with words, and an eagerness to learn with an atmosphere that would enable him to go on from there.

Problems remained. He was still a family man, for he had not broken with Cornelia, although his recent behavior had placed a strain on their marriage; he knew that he was not entirely free, either to follow his fancy or to be entirely honest. The change was primarily one of emphasis. The myth of the abrupt break still persists, but it is not far from the essence of the truth. Anderson had rejected the standards of the market place and had set off to find his own.

2

THE BEGINNING OF THE SEARCH

T HE years following Sherwood Anderson's return to Chicago, from early 1913 through 1919, comprised the most important period in his life. Entering it as an unknown with vaguely defined protests against modern American materialism, a few rough manuscripts, and the urge to write, he emerged a promising writer who had come close to the essence of human experience. During these years he produced two novels, the early manuscripts of which he had brought with him; a book of free verse chants; and a collection of integrated short stories.

Anderson's own experiences provided the raw material for much of his work as well as for the material of this first creative period. More important, they presented the problems that were at the core of the lifelong search that he began in Elyria to understand American life. At first these problems were intensely personal ones: the meaning of his father's life and his own relation to it; the problem of human isolation he had seen personified in the life of his mother; the secret behind the human love that seemed so much at the mercy of outside economic and materialistic forces; and the problem of personal identity. These problems were, however, as Anderson was to learn, manifestations of universal problems made more intense by the forces that had come to dominate the American consciousness during his own lifetime.

Anderson's desire to write of these problems and to understand them was much more than a mere wish; it dominated his life so completely that at a time when he could have been sliding easily into a comfortable middle age, he changed the course of his life. In advertising he had a place of retreat as well as a means of earning a living, but he maintained only a loose tie with it. His goal was to write and to understand his world and his life; what he needed was direction that would give form to his tentative efforts. The literary renaissance in Chicago provided that direction as well as the sympathy, encouragement, and stimulation he needed.

The Chicago literary renaissance has been described by Bernard Duffey, who terms it a movement of liberation that was to have lasting effects on American literature.[1] For Anderson the movement provided an introduction to Gertrude Stein's *Tender Buttons*, given him by his brother Karl, and the opportunity, through the 57th Street artistic colony, to seek out his own means of expression through an intimate knowledge of himself. The impact of the revolutionary nature of the Stein volume was so great that he remembered it all his life as a revelation that he might be able to produce a style of his own; it opened possibilities undreamed of by him in Elyria. Although his first published short story, "The Rabbit-Pen," which appeared in *Harper's* in July 1914, was an innocuous piece that showed little of what was to come, it did bring him respect and encouragement from his new friends.

To follow up his minor success in *Harper's*, Anderson was trying to do something with the two novel manuscripts he had brought with him from Elyria. It is impossible to tell how much work he did on them in Chicago, but in scope if not in final form they must have remained essentially unchanged. In both, the protagonists find fulfillment in the act of rebellion against materialistic standards; and after rebellion each finds nothing except a vague satisfaction in physical intimacy with others and in determined efforts to find spiritual intimacy. Both points are reminiscent of Anderson's earlier efforts at attaining "commercial democracy," and both novels are autobiographical. The first of them, *Windy McPherson's Son*, is factually so, and the second, *Marching Men*, portrays Anderson the reformer as he saw himself after his world of commerce became meaningless in Elyria.

Windy McPherson's Son was published in 1916 by the John Lane Company of London. As a novel it contains little of absolute value. Its real significances are that it demonstrates Anderson's ability to recapture the essence of seemingly meaningless incidents in brief sketches and that it recapitulates the theme that was to dominate his life work: the search for human values and meaning in a materialistic world.

Essentially, the story is a simple one, recounting Anderson's own

[1] Bernard Duffey, *The Chicago Renaissance in American Letters* (East Lansing: Michigan State College Press, 1954), p. 261.

life up to his rejection of materialistic standards in Elyria. In the novel, a poor boy from a small town, through hard work and sharp dealing, rises to a position of wealth and responsibility. Later, he learns painfully that money isn't everything. Such a story is far from new, as Anderson realized later, but in Elyria it was both new and heretical to him. The protagonist of the novel, Sam McPherson, is clearly Anderson himself, and Sam's family, especially his father and his mother, are drawn from Anderson's life, as are the settings of the small Midwestern town of Caxton and the metropolis of Chicago. The raw material of the story is the personal experience that Anderson was trying to understand.

Together with his ambition, Sam has a curiosity that becomes almost a hunger for insight into the meaning of the lives around him. The two are incompatible, and Sam loses sight of the latter as he pursues the material success that seems so attractive. By his eagerness to work and succeed, Sam earns modest success as a trader in his home town, as well as the nickname "Jobby"; he then goes to Chicago, where, through hard work, thrift, and sharp dealing that he had learned in Caxton, he rises to the top of the armament industry. In the process he subordinates all his human instincts to his goal, and in the finest Horatio Alger tradition he marries the boss's daughter.

Suddenly Sam's success becomes meaningless when his wife leaves him and his father-in-law commits suicide. Finding himself completely alone and realizing that he has sacrificed human beings for things, Sam decides to abandon his business affairs to try to find the human feeling he has lost. After a series of adventures as a laborer, an anonymous benefactor of a small town, an altruistic strike leader, and a frustrated playboy, he realizes that these efforts are futile and that he must take a different direction. When he meets a woman who wishes to be rid of her children, he takes them home to his wife, and together they decide to build a new life based on love.

This outline indicates the parallel between Anderson's life and that of his protagonist; it also indicates the nature of the problems that made Anderson turn to writing in the attempt to understand the world he had been caught up in. The most important of these is the problem of human isolation, which dominates the book, just as it had dominated Anderson's life in Elyria. Early in the novel the problem is presented in three characters: in Sam's father, Windy;

in his mother; and in John Telfer, a wealthy, educated man of the town who befriends Sam.

The figure of Windy McPherson is central to the story, although Sam leaves him behind as inconsequential when he leaves Caxton. Windy is unable to separate reality from imagination. In the town he is a failure, as was Irwin Anderson, and many critics interpret this portrayal as a vicious portrait of Anderson's own father. It is a real but not a condemning portrait, however, and it reveals much insight into Irwin's problems. Windy is a man completely isolated from his wife, his children, and his contemporaries, but Anderson does not condemn the man who does not belong; rather, he draws him as he was seen by the times, a lazy liar rather than a wandering storyteller and a craftsman. Sam, in spite of his later realization that he, too, is isolated from his fellow humans, never understands his father; for Anderson, on the other hand, this is the first of many attempts to know Irwin.

Feeling shame and disgust for his father, Sam is drawn closer to his mother, but here he again faces something he is unable to understand: a love that finds its only expression in service. Completely dominated by her necessity to keep the family together and fed, Sam's mother is overworked, sickly, and inarticulate. Yet her love for her children is shown in a series of incidents marked by her self-sacrifice. This is the love that Sam later tries to recapture and understand, but he fails in his efforts to put it into practice after his rejection of business ethics.

Outside his own family Sam is drawn to John Telfer, a wealthy idler about the town, who combines the qualities that Sam most desires for himself: leisure and money as well as the ability to appreciate the luxuries of art and ideas. Telfer tells Sam that

> ". . . in our day money-making precedes many virtues that are forever on men's lips . . . money makes life livable. It gives freedom and destroys fear. Having it means sanitary houses and well-made clothes. It brings into men's lives beauty and the love of beauty. It enables a man to go adventuring after the stuff of life as I have done."

Sam accepts Telfer's words completely, ignoring the man's true position in the town. Telfer is the symbol of the materialistic future, no less anachronistic than Windy and no less isolated. Because of his wealth and his education, he is feared and respected in the town, but he is not loved. As the local apostle of the new materialism, he is admired by Sam, who does not see that Telfer has neither humanity nor human feeling.

In accepting Telfer's philosophy, Sam cuts himself off from human love, and the last part of the novel is devoted to his efforts to break through the resulting barriers he had erected. In a moment of despair after his rejection, he implores,

> "Are you there, O God? Have you left your children here on the earth hurting each other? Do you put the seed of a million children in a man, and the planting of a forest in one tree, and permit men to wreck and hurt and destroy?"

Later, at the end, he resolves that, "I cannot run away from life. I must face it. I must try to understand these other lives, to love."

Out of this theme of human isolation Anderson draws these conclusions: he portrays industrial and business ethics as dehumanizing; he shows that man has lost all concepts of meaning in a society dominated by superficiality; and he points out that man has lost awareness of himself as a natural human being. That these were in themselves problems crying for solution Anderson seems not to recognize in the novel; rather, he implies that the act of rejection of materialistic standards, replaced by a determination to understand life and to love, is almost sufficient in itself to break down the barriers of human isolation and to nullify these subsidiary problems. That rejection is not an answer but merely a beginning of the search for an answer, Anderson knew well from his own experience; but because he had no idea of what came after that rejection, he sought in the novel a simplified solution in a simple event. But the situation was far more complex than he realized, and the ending is as indecisive as Anderson himself was in Elyria.

As a first novel *Windy McPherson's Son* has strengths and weaknesses. The shortcomings in the novel are so numerous that they tend to obscure its merits. Dialogue is stilted, rhetorical, and unnatural; didacticism appears all too frequently. The well-drawn portraits and sketches in the early portion devoted to the small town are overwhelmed by the unreality of Sam's careers as tycoon and as wanderer. Stylistically, the novel is self-conscious, naive, and contrived, giving little indication of Anderson's later artistic powers. Today the story seems dated; yet, in spite of these shortcomings the significance of the novel as a portrayal of rejection and of search reflects the pattern of Anderson's life up to that time.

Critical reception of the novel was generally favorable, and Anderson's prestige among the Chicago group rose accordingly, giving him enough confidence to branch out in the new literary directions inspired by his Chicago contacts. Meanwhile, he brought out his second novel, *Marching Men,* also written as an attempt to find an answer to the conflict between the individual and his world. In this novel, however, Anderson shifts his focus from a protagonist who has risen to the top of the materialistic world only to find it meaningless, to one who by choice remains at its lowest levels, aligning himself with those exploited by the system.

In *Marching Men* Anderson has again written an autobiographical novel, but it is autobiography of a different sort. Instead of dealing with fictionalized fact, Anderson bases the novel on fictionalized fancy like that which engendered his "commercial democracy" movement, his "secret" book "Why I Am a Socialist," and his efforts to find an answer to the problem of what one should do after he has rebelled. After finishing *Windy McPherson's Son,* he concluded that a course of positive action was needed, and he conceived *Marching Men* to satisfy that need. However, the solution he sets forth in this book was also predestined to failure, as he realized after he recognized the complexity of the social and economic structure he was trying to reform in one easy swoop.

Beaut McGregor, the protagonist of *Marching Men,* is essentially like Sam McPherson in his determination to make his presence felt in the world, but there is one major difference. Sam was motivated by faith in the traditional American virtues, but Beaut is driven by his hatred for the people in the little Pennsylvania mining town in which he was raised, people who are stupid enough to go into "the black hole between the Pennsylvania hills" and dig coal. Early in the novel he muses on the words of the town socialist

who was forever talking of a day coming when men would march shoulder to shoulder and life in Coal Creek, life everywhere, should cease being aimless and become definite and full of meaning.

If men ever did march together, Beaut reflected, they were so stupid that he would march them to an abandoned mine cut and push them in.

Beaut's bitterness results from his father's death in an abandoned mine shaft, and is intensified because of a strike in which his mother, owner of a small bakery, goes bankrupt feeding the miners. During the strike he is fascinated by the soldiers who marched through the streets restoring order. Full of hate, he then goes to Chicago to seek his fortune, convinced that he must take what he wants if he is to succeed in life. Later, while studying law, he realizes that "Brains are intended to help fists!"

At this point Beaut's career parallels Sam McPherson's, but again a significant difference is evident. While Sam saw life as a game, with the rewards going to the quickest, the most able, and the shrewdest, Beaut sees it as a vicious battle, with the victory going to the strongest and the most unscrupulous. While *Windy Mc-Pherson's Son* reflects Anderson's disillusionment with the world of commerce, *Marching Men* shows his bitterness at it and his willingness to fight it on its own terms, matching brute strength against animal savagery and cunning.

However, Beaut's hatred shifts to the exploiting employers when his mother's death demonstrates to him the love and loyalty that the miners hold for her, and he learns to love them in return. Determined to lead them out of their misery, Beaut fuses his love, his desire for their freedom and dignity, and his concept of men marching solidly together, imbues the result with his recognition of the savage nature of the materialistic structure, and then dreams up the marching men movement.

The movement is force personified, taking its strength from the mass of men who made up its body; and again, as in the conclusion of *Windy McPherson's Son*, Anderson is faced with a dilemma: after the movement, what? After force has defeated force, is there any hope for the individual anyway, or will he be destroyed forever by the dehumanizing forces that were set in motion to save him? Anderson is unable to answer the question, and the novel concludes with the implication that the movement is doomed and that Beaut will go down with it, still fighting.

In spite of the often-noted weakness of the second half of the novel, however, certain significant factors are apparent. First, Anderson had made a headlong attack on the basic problem that concerned him, the dehumanizing effects of the new materialism; and in doing so he learned that there was no easy solution, that he could not adapt its own weapons to a fight against it without in the end compounding the evil. It was this kind of realization, more than any other, that later prevented him from going over to communism when he was attracted to it.

Anderson also learned from writing this novel that there is no gimmick by which to solve the problem of human isolation. Although in his army days he had felt himself to be one of the boys as they marched together toward an objective, he now saw danger in such a movement. Shoulders touching did not mean that men's souls were in harmony, as he later pointed out in *A Story Teller's Story,* and a mass movement is too easily dominated by instincts rejected by the individual conscience.

Finally, the conclusion makes a significant point that reveals Anderson's conception of the only meaningful road for man: the belief that man can never triumph over his materialistic environment, that he can only resist it. As the novel closes, Beaut's counterpart among the industrialists, Ormsby, a rich plow manufacturer, says:

> . . . perhaps McGregor knew he would fail and yet had the courage of failure. . . . What if after all this McGregor and his woman knew both roads? What if they, after looking deliberately along the road toward success in life, went without regret along the road to failure? What if McGregor and not myself knew the road to beauty?

Perhaps this is merely a rationalization and an ennobling of Anderson's decision at the end of his Elyria years to reject business success and to follow his drive to write and to understand. However, the recurrence of deliberately chosen failure in the conclusions of his later works indicates that it is more: Anderson sees the ultimate end of man as tragic, and any meaning inherent in life can lie only in the way it is lived. Therefore, life is good only if it is expended in a cause worth dying for.

The marching men movement does not contain the overtones of Fascism that critics of the 1930s read into it. It was supposed to instill loyalty among men on every level and eliminate distrust, fighting, and petty differences. A spiritual affinity would arise that would remove all barriers between men. Men would be able to achieve meaning, dignity, and fulfillment through close association with their fellows; and their surface unity would indicate the depth of their spiritual unity. Taken on the surface, this was an extreme assumption that offered a simple and impossible solution to a complex and perhaps unsolvable problem. However, it was far from totalitarian in its conception.

Other weaknesses are apparent in the book. As in *Windy Mc-*

Pherson's Son, dialogue is stilted, and unnatural rhetorical flourishes abound. Characterization tends to be stereotyped, with the single exception of Ormsby, the plow manufacturer. However, in *Marching Men,* Anderson has advanced in his ideological viewpoint to the realization that there is no easy solution to life's problems. Truth, therefore, must lie in another direction: in people rather than in circumstances.

Marching Men also marks a stylistic advance. In several instances Anderson permits himself the indulgence of a release of free-verse-like rhythms, notably in the arbitrarily inserted passage on Chicago. He writes:

> And back of Chicago lie the long corn fields that are not disorderly. There is hope in the corn. Spring comes and the corn is green. It shoots up out of the black land and stands up in orderly rows. The corn grows and thinks of nothing but growth. . . .
>
> And Chicago has forgotten the lesson of the corn. All men have forgotten. It has never been told to the young men who come out of the corn fields to live in the city.

In the context of the novel, this passage is self-conscious and naive as well as jarring in sentiment and style, probably an early product of the impact of the Chicago experiences, inserted in the process of revision. It does, however, point out Anderson's forthcoming attempt in *Mid-American Chants* to find a natural style of his own, as well as his attempt in that work to return ideologically to enduring aspects of the American environment. Here, however, is Anderson's first conscious effort to put into practice the discovery made through the Chicago renaissance: that a writer must find himself, his subject matter, and his own means of expression rather than imitate others.

With the publication of *Marching Men* Anderson ended one phase of his literary career and tentatively began another. The first two novels, *Windy McPherson's Son* and *Marching Men,* had been the voice of the disillusioned businessman trying to explain to himself the causes of his disenchantment and to propose a panacea for America's ills. If he had remained in Elyria after this point, content to have put his ideas and his dreams on paper and then to settle back in despair if they were ignored, he might have become another Irwin Anderson or Windy McPherson. But two factors combined to prevent this circumstance. One was Anderson's fascination with the power of words, stemming from his early experiences at Wittenberg and in advertising and intensified by the evenings spent reading at the Anderson home. The other was the influence of the Chicago years.

While he was attempting to find a publisher for *Windy Mc-Pherson's Son* and *Marching Men,* Anderson began to regard himself as a writer rather than as a businessman-amateur or as a parlor radical trying to undermine the status quo. Two other products of the Elyria years, the manuscripts of the novels "Mary Cochran" and "Talbot Whittingham," were put aside, never to be published, except in fragments, and he began to see writing as an artistic end in itself rather than as a means to communicate, to convince, or to sell either goods or ideas.

The rapidity with which Anderson assimilated the atmosphere of personal and artistic liberation exuded by Gertrude Stein and his new associates is indicated by the appearance of a brief essay of his in the first issue of Margaret Anderson's *Little Review,* the voice of the Chicago literary renaissance. In this essay, entitled "The New Note," Anderson combines instinctively perceived facts about writing and about life with the belief in self-expression and self-trust emphasized by the Chicago liberation, and he proclaims a philosophy of writing that was to dominate his career to the end. In terms remarkable for their self-confidence after the doubt and indecision that had plagued him in Elyria, he writes:

> In the trade of writing the so-called new note is as old as the world. Simply stated, it is a cry for the reinjection of truth and honesty into the craft . . . . it is an appeal from the standards set up by money-making magazine and book publishers . . . to the older, sweeter standards of the craft itself. . . .

This is a mere rephrasing of the standards Anderson had advocated in the advertising copy written in Cleveland, adapted from the business world to the literary, and as such it is nothing new. Rather, it indicates his determination not to let his new career be contaminated, as was the old. In writing, he had found an area in which he could put into practice the principles of honesty that seemed to have no place in the business world. From this basis the rest of the essay turns to the new spirit of self-expression released by the liberation:

. . . In the love of his craft he [the writer] has done the most difficult of all things: revealed the workings of his own soul and mind. . . . Whenever he finds himself baffled in drawing a character or in judging one drawn by another, let him turn thus in upon himself, trusting with child-like simplicity and honesty the truth that lives in his own mind.

Thus armed with a faith that was to provide the basis for the rest of his literary career, Anderson embarked upon his new, consciously chosen career. He was still married at this time and still earned his living as an advertising writer, but these remnants of an earlier existence had nothing to do with the sense of liberation that he gained from the Chicago experience.

His marriage with Cornelia had been seriously strained when he left Elyria, and although she brought the children to Chicago, the marriage had been damaged irreparably. Cornelia had tried to accept the new Anderson with good grace, even contributing a book review to the first issue of the *Little Review,* but the marriage could not last. In the fall of 1915 they were divorced, an event about which Anderson chose to remain almost silent in his published memoirs, although he and Cornelia remained on good terms. Later he commented that ". . . it was this feeling of dirt in life, in myself, that had destroyed my relations with my family."

Entering wholeheartedly into the spirit of the Chicago liberation, Anderson became markedly colorful and unconventional, wearing loud socks and scarves instead of neckties. Moreover, even before his divorce he spent the summer of 1915 at Lake Chateaugay, New York, with Tennessee Mitchell, a small-town Michigan girl turned musician, dancer, sculptress, and the epitome of the newly emancipated woman. Later, in 1916, he married her, inaugurating a relationship designed, in keeping with the spirit of liberation, to place responsibility on neither person. The Chicago period was the only time when Anderson led what is conventionally considered to be a Bohemian life. Anderson, Cornelia, and Tennessee remained on good terms even after Cornelia took a teaching job in Indiana, and the three of them, with the children, vacationed together in 1916.

At the time that Anderson broke with Cornelia, he also broke literary ties with his earlier works and took a direction wholly new and unrestrained, both in fiction and in what was for him the new field of verse lyricism. The former eventually resulted in *Winesburg, Ohio,* and the latter made up his next book, *Mid-American*

Chants, the last of the three volumes required by his contract with John Lane.

Mid-American Chants contains the first fruits of the literary freedom he had experienced in Chicago. Written in late 1914 and early 1915, the verses illustrate the transition from his earlier effort to write in a self-consciously literary and rhetorical style that had nothing to do with his own Midwestern personality to a no less self-conscious effort to rid his writing of "literariness," allowing it to seek its own natural rhythms. Consequently, in the same sense that the earlier works are the thematic forerunners of Anderson's later works, the *Chants* are the stylistic sources from which they evolve.

A change in purpose is also significantly evident in the *Chants.* No longer interested in selling ideas, he is earnestly trying to convey to his reader moments of feeling, of emotion, and of what he feels is insight. His purpose, as he states in the foreword of the slender volume, is to sound a note of affirmation in the American scene, to explore and celebrate the ". . . few memory haunted places" that have been hidden by the coal piles and slag heaps of an industrial civilization, hoping that in the process he can set free the spirit of the American people.

The resulting collection of verse is so free and so unformed that it becomes not only trying, but tiresome. As verse, it is insignificant, but from the point of view of Anderson's literary and thematic development it is the most important of his earlier works. The two-fold shift—in style and in regarding his native experiences as meaningful and worthwhile—lays the groundwork for the outstanding short stories that follow the book; hence, in a very real sense the new freedom made it possible for him to discover himself both as writer and as interpreter of the Midwestern experience.

Indications of his newly found freedom abound in the volume, much of it out of place in what is supposed to be pure and spontaneous lyricism. Sometimes, however, it seems peculiarly right as he feels his way toward the essence of Midwestern sentiment expressed in its native idiom. For example, in "Song of Industrial America" he writes, "Now here's how it's going to come—the song, I mean. I've watched things, men and faces—I know." He continues:

> First there are the broken things—myself and the others. I don't mind that—I'm gone—shot to pieces. I'm part of the scheme—I'm the broken end of a song myself . . . Now, faint voices do lift up.

They are swept away in the void—that's true enough. It had to be so from the very first. Pshaw—I'm steady enough—let me alone. Keokuk, Tennessee, Michigan, Chicago, Kalamazoo—don't the names in this country make you fairly drunk? We'll stand by this brown stream for hours. I'll not be swept away. Watch my hand—how steady it is. To catch this song and sing it would do much—make much clear.

Taken out of the arbitrary arrangement in which they were published, verses such as these are not poetry by any stretch of the imagination; they do, however, belong to a much older tradition— the tradition of the oral storyteller whose purpose was to seek and to hold the attention of his listeners while he found his way to the point he was trying to make. This is the tradition of the Middle West of the eighties and nineties, when the countless counterparts of Irwin Anderson were holding forth in harness shops, general stores, and barber shops scattered across the rural countryside. When Anderson turned his writing loose to seek its own style, it turned instinctively to that tradition. Often exasperating in its meandering and hence unsatisfactory to a reader accustomed to crisp directness, it is nevertheless a true rendition of a native Midwestern technique that is not studiously correct but spontaneous, unsophisticated, and honest. It is a style that would naturally attract a man who was tired of dishonesty, artificiality, and trickery in the use of words as well as in normal human affairs.

Contrasted to this are instances in which the speech is forced and unnatural, stemming from efforts to be poetically profound in such passages as, "Into the cities my people had gathered. They had become dizzy with words. Words choked them. They could not breathe." But even here the artificial sonorousness is punctuated by the hard, direct language of a rural people. Words like "dizzy" and "choked" are hardly poetic, but they are both functional and right for the people and the places to which Anderson was to devote himself. Here, in the *Chants*, in a medium to which it is not suited, the attempt to reproduce an oral tradition results in a markedly naive and unsuccessful literary effort. But as Anderson was to show in his later works, the reproduction becomes successful when consciously adapted to the form from which it was derived and for which it is most suited—the short tale.

Together with innovations in style, a second major shift in direction is also significant in the *Chants*. In both of his earlier novels

Anderson had been so overwhelmed by the evils he was trying to combat that he could see nothing else. The rural countryside, the peaceful atmosphere of the small town, the order, beauty, and fertility of a field of growing corn were ignored by the young man on the make and by the hater devoted to crushing the thing that he hated. In the freedom of this volume Anderson allows himself to pause, to look around, and to see that in spite of the industrial monster dominating the American scene, there is much untouched by it that is both good and enduring. He has not forgotten industrialism; it concurrently fascinates him and repels him, recurring in the imagery of verses like "Song to New Song," sung in the face of fiery furnaces, coal heaps, and a sky black with smoke. Industrialism exists, but it is unimportant in the light of the important things that the poet has neglected and to which he now wants to return.

This re-examination makes up the major theme of the volume. In "The Cornfields" he sets up his purpose, to call to attention the health, vitality, and fertility that America possesses but has lost sight of; "Song of Industrial America" carries the idea further by focusing on the place names man had given to the natural setting— names evocative of the natural strengths and human lives behind them. All of this, he feels, has been ignored and must be revived. Even beyond this, Anderson proclaims that we are one with our past and our environment and that we must recognize this kinship. In "Song of Cedric the Silent" Anderson bridges the gaps between the mystic past and the living present by proclaiming spiritual unity in a manner adopted from Whitman's "Song of Myself." Throughout the *Chants* Anderson celebrates whatever he sees to be right and natural, couching much of this theme, as in his "Song of Theodore," in the sexual symbolism used by Walt Whitman. Corn is no longer viewed as a symbol of order, as it was in the brief passage in *Marching Men,* but as a symbol of fertility inherent in America, waiting to be discovered by those who would seek it out. Anderson's almost Biblically couched affirmation that the people and the earth exist and that they are good is a further indication of his concept of spiritual unity. He concludes the volume with "Evening Song" and "Song of the Singer," in both of which he returns to the open fields that hold so much promise, and then defies the might of the industrial machine. In the former he proclaims his hope and trust in the Midwestern countryside; in the latter he affirms his faith.

Mid-American Chants is a book Anderson had to write. At the conclusion of *Marching Men* he acknowledged that a frontal assault on the forces of materialism was futile and that humanism could not win without giving up its essence and becoming what it tried to destroy. Yet he ended on a note of faith, as he had in *Windy McPherson's Son*. Somewhere, he knew, there was something that would instill meaning into lives and break down the barriers between them, but neither desire, no matter how strong, nor action, no matter how sustained, could do it. One thing remained: to probe into the American consciousness, to find what was true, and to make the truth known. In effect he was doing what Sam McPherson set out to do in his wandering, to discover for himself what was lasting in America. But in *Mid-American Chants* he was not trying to do it by direct action, as businessmen McPherson and Anderson had been trained to do; rather, instead of cures he is seeking understanding. If he is successful, the walls between people will not be demolished by brute force, but will be undermined and will collapse of their own weight. *Mid-American Chants* marks this change in approach, essentially for Anderson a change from reformer and propagandist to artist.

As a book of verse, *Mid-American Chants* is, as Bernard Duffey comments, "as bad a case of maundering and abortive work as the whole Chicago Liberation, so ready in formless effusion, was to produce." [2] Liberty had been too readily interpreted as license by Anderson as well as by his colleagues, and although the resulting free verse that is more prose than poetry had shown Anderson the way to reproduce the flat, meandering Midwestern idiom, thereby creating a new literary style, it did not result in the lyricism that was intended. Rather it resulted in awkwardness, repetitiousness, and monotony instead of spontaneous expression. From an artistic point of view the book as a whole is a failure, the few genuine lyrics in it insufficient to redeem it. However, from the point of view of Anderson's literary development, it was a success, for in it Anderson had discovered both himself and his material. No longer seeking fulfillment either in rebellion or in propagandizing against the forces he hated and feared, he began to seek it in a conscious effort to know, understand, and embrace his own Midwest and the people who make it live.

Even while he was releasing himself in unrestrained and undis-

[2] Duffey, *The Chicago Renaissance*, p. 203.

ciplined lyricism in the verses that were to become *Mid-American Chants,* Anderson's newly awakened sensitivity toward the psychological and spiritual depths of man became evident in the short fiction that he wrote between 1914 and 1916. "The Rabbit-Pen," an attempt to fuse the symbolism of a buck rabbit running wild in his pen with the improbable love affair of a writer, is perhaps a product of the Elyria years, and as such is artificial and contrived. However, two of his early stories in the *Little Review* show an abrupt change.

The first of these, "Sister," published in December 1915, shows a complete rejection of the heavy-handed, contrived symbolism of "The Rabbit-Pen." A sketch rather than a story, "Sister" is an attempted allegory in which the narrator tells of his sister, an artist, who is beaten by their father because she admits that she plans to have an affair in order to experience physical love. The style is impressionistic, like that of the poems in *Chants,* but the symbolism is inconsistent; the narrator is first the world and then a worker of the world who fears that the world will destroy his sister. The conclusion is a vague fear that the world will destroy the artist although she has a right to be destroyed.

Nevertheless "Sister" is an important link between the impressionistic exuberance of *Chants* and the artistically controlled unity of the stories in *Winesburg, Ohio*. In the story, Anderson has successfully adapted the free, colloquial rhythms of the verse to prose, accurately and forcefully reproducing the patterns of narrative speech; he has also subordinated those patterns to a pre-determined effect. At the same time he has emphasized psychological insight into human brutality as he moves from the objectively real world, characterized by a beating administered in a house on North Dearborn Street in Chicago, to the world of symbolic universality. In spite of its weaknesses, "Sister," like the poems, is an experimental ancestor of Anderson's later successful stories.

The story "Vibrant Life," published in March 1916, is a semi-autobiographical attempt to lay bare the essence of a man who breaks away from convention only to find himself trapped again. Finally, in a macabre scene, the protagonist attacks a young woman who is sitting up with him at the wake of his dead brother. As he wrestles with the girl, they upset the coffin. It breaks open, the body rolls to the floor, and the protagonist leers triumphantly at the young woman. Although the story is fantastic and the symbolism leaden and awkward, it shows the destruction of convention and sexual repression. Despite its flaws, "Vibrant Life" is a step closer to the stories of *Winesburg, Ohio.* Increasingly, Anderson was becoming interested in the inner nature of human life—the twists, the quirks, and the secrets that make communication between individuals so difficult; and he was moving slowly in the direction that would bring them to light in his work. The short fiction of this period provided the apprenticeship in form that he needed, just as the inadequate solutions in his novels made him introspective and as the *Chants* taught him that he possessed both a style and an increasingly trustworthy perceptiveness.

The importance of the influence of Gertrude Stein and of the Chicago liberation group on Anderson's work during these years cannot be overemphasized, but other factors were also at work. One of these was his awakened interest in painting, not as a means of expression but because of his interest in color and in the endless possibilities for effect provided by color. As art, his canvasses were inconsequential (although the Radical Book Shop later gave him a one-man show), and Anderson was not deluded into thinking otherwise. But the possibilities inherent in color indicated to him the equally endless potentialities inherent in the words of his own craft.

Another influence of this period was his discovery of the rhythmic cadences of the Bible. In it he found the effect that he had been trying to secure in his own experimental work. One day Anderson startled the copy room at the advertising agency by announcing that he "was sold on Jesus Christ," by which he meant the poetry he found in the New Testament. He wrote a number of prose poems in which he tried deliberately to capture the Biblical style.

At this point, his friendship with Trigant Burrow, a pioneer psychoanalyst, brought into sharper focus his increasing interest in the inner workings of the human mind. He had met Burrow during the summer of 1915, and a close friendship developed. However, Anderson was not interested in curing ills, but in understanding the ills as well as the strengths of the human heart; and although he approached psychoanalytical techniques in many characterizations, he relied primarily on his own intuition to ferret out the essence of human character.

During the time when these influences were most active, in late 1915 and throughout 1916, he had begun to work on the stories that were to make up *Winesburg, Ohio,* but as yet he had no idea of

their potential as an organized whole. At the same time he was
straining at the ties that held him to Chicago. His advertising work
had become almost free-lance, and the liberation group was breaking
up as its members began to drift to New York. The early volumes
had brought him some reputation and respect in the East, and he
began to look in that direction, spending more and more time out
of Chicago until he began a period of restless wandering that lasted
for most of the 1920s.

As the publication of *Winesburg, Ohio* approached, it can be seen
that Anderson had come a long way from the frustrated and em-
bittered businessman who was trying to find personal fulfillment and
meaning by condemning and attacking the American business and
industrial civilization. He was a promising writer with three published books behind him and an enthusiastic, if small, audience
awaiting his next work. At this point he had found himself as an honest
writer-craftsman; he had found the beginnings of a style that was
to reflect both himself and the Midwestern world of which he realized he was intrinsically a part. He had also found that, beneath the
seeming meaninglessness and ugliness of the industrial and commercial surface of America, there was still a solid core that was
worthwhile. From Sam McPherson's abortive efforts to love without
understanding, he had learned that understanding and compassion
had to precede love, and in the *Winesburg, Ohio* stories he was to
find all three. In this book he once more plunged headlong into the
problem of the isolation of the individual human being, but in writing it he was not a frustrated polemicist; he was a conscious literary
artist.

3

MOMENTS OF INSIGHT

IN 1919 Sherwood Anderson published *Winesburg, Ohio,* a collection of short stories and sketches written between late 1915 and late 1917. This book contains many parallels to Anderson's earlier works: in subject matter Anderson returns to the small Midwestern town that had provided the background for the earlier parts of *Windy McPherson's Son;* in theme he re-examines isolation of the individual; and in technique he combines his natural Midwestern style and the short form with which he had been experimenting in the short stories published in the *Little Review.* But to say that Anderson merely combined all these factors and emerged with a major literary achievement is an oversimplification; the literary apprenticeship that he served was long, painful, and determined.

Anderson himself attempted to account for the abrupt shift from mediocre to substantial achievement several times, most recently in his *Memoirs.* He stated that the first of the stories, "Hands," was written in its entirety at one sitting as the result of a moment of intense emotional excitement. For days he had been sitting at his boardinghouse-room window, watching people pass by. "Somehow it had seemed to me . . . that each person who passed along the street below . . . shouted his secret up to me. I was myself and still I fled out of myself. It seemed to me that I went into the others."

This must have been just before or shortly after he had completed *Mid-American Chants.* At this time he was "trying for something. To escape out of old minds, old thoughts put into my head by others, into my own thoughts, my own feelings." Previously, in keeping with the spirit of the Chicago liberation, he had tried to look into his own heart and to understand others through himself, as he had emphasized in "The New Note." Now he wanted to go farther:

> To at last go out of myself, truly into others, the others I met
> constantly in the streets of the city, in the office where I then

worked, and still others, remembered out of my childhood in an American small town.

Suddenly he went to his table and wrote, finishing "Hands" at one sitting, knowing when he had finished that it was right, that he had captured the essence of ". . . a poor little man, beaten, pounded, frightened by the world in which he lived into something oddly beautiful." When he knew that it was right, he knew also that he had found both himself and his vocation, "Getting for the first time belief in self." In the succeeding days and weeks he finished the rest of the stories, writing furiously in his room, at work, or wherever he could find a moment.

Whether this account is factually correct or not really does not matter. What does matter is that Anderson had attained artistic insight in a form eminently suited to his own peculiar talents for attaining empathy. Such empathy is the product of an intensely emotional and often fleeting moment, and it cannot be sustained for long periods, certainly not long enough to develop character in a novel. But in the short sketches and stories of *Winesburg, Ohio,* it produced superb results. In the intensity of these moments of understanding, Anderson could fuse sympathy with insight and lyrical excitement and lose consciousness of himself as he wrote.

It is this ability to lose consciousness of oneself that contains the key to Sherwood Anderson's achievement in *Winesburg, Ohio.* In his earlier works Anderson had been dealing with himself: directly in his portrayal of Sam McPherson and vicariously in the figure of Beaut McGregor. But his experiment in *Mid-American Chants* had shown him that mere personal experience is not enough, that there is an undefined but real quality needed to transmute that experience into literature. In *Winesburg, Ohio* he uses his experience as a point of departure, but he goes beyond it in search of that elusive quality.

✱ Here he deals with human lives other than his own, but he is not content to see them in relation to himself. Instead he catches each of them at an essential moment in time that reveals a series of brief, intuitive, but true glimpses of the anguish of the human heart. Each story reveals the essence of the central character's life as Anderson knows it.

The fact that these moments of insight are presented in the volume as an integrated whole creates a problem in defining the volume according to one of the convenient literary genres. It has been called both a novel and a collection of short stories and sketches. Anderson himself always referred to each element as a story or a tale, but he considered the book as a whole to be a novel—a novel form he had invented. In his *Memoirs* he stated that:

> I have even sometimes thought that the novel form does not fit an American writer, that it is a form which had been brought in. What is wanted is a new looseness; and in *Winesburg* I have made my own form. There were individual tales but all about lives in some way connected. . . . Life is a loose flowing thing.

Whether this form was a conscious contrivance at the time, as Anderson indicates it was, or whether it was merely a convenience makes very little difference. The form is loose; there are elements both within the stories and in the book's organization and theme that draw the tales together; but within this unity there is a great deal of diversity in the many lives portrayed, each differing from the others and all different from Anderson's own. The result is Anderson's first work that is undeniably both fiction and literature.

The common background of the stories has contributed to a number of mistaken interpretations of *Winesburg, Ohio*, the most common being that Anderson is showing a cross section of a small town, revealing its secret sins in such detail that he is in effect "revolting from the village." This generality has endured in spite of the fact that it is far from what Anderson had intended or accomplished. He was not attacking the small town or its mores; rather he was writing about people as they might be found anywhere, and was exploring deeply and in detail individual human lives. That the people he portrays are not unique to either small town or city but common to both is shown by his statement that the characterizations came from ". . . everywhere about me, in towns in which I had lived, in the army, in factories and offices." They represent the people of Clyde, Chicago, and Elyria, and *Winesburg, Ohio* is a composite that draws its substance from all of Anderson's experience.

In the book, Anderson is exploring the problem of human isolation; but he does not approach the problem with the sweeping condemnation of society and industrialism, as he did in *Windy McPherson's Son* and *Marching Men*. Anderson had learned, as he implied in *Marching Men*, that isolation is not merely a product of modern materialism. Isolation originates in a narrowness of human vision and in an inability or, in some cases, an unwillingness to attempt to understand the complexities of human life and experience. His earlier protagonists had been fumbling their way toward this understanding, but they sought it in rejection. He learned from *Marching Men* that isolation can neither be cured by an all-embracing remedy based on the appearance of understanding; nor can it be understood by the mere desire to understand, as *Windy McPherson's Son* taught him.

In the short stories of *Winesburg, Ohio,* Anderson is determined to treat isolation as a phenomenon of the individual rather than as a manifestation of a social evil. As such, he approached the problem on its simplest level, seeking understanding through intuitive perception. This was to be accomplished not through analysis, but through empathy, his purpose being not to diagnose and to cure, but simply to understand and to love. The stories are not from the couch of a literary psychiatrist; they are vehicles by which Anderson as craftsman can explore the human soul.

In the first of the sketches, "The Book of the Grotesque," which Anderson uses as a statement of purpose, this approach is defined in symbolic terms. He shows that the individuals in the stories have been so twisted psychologically that their real natures have little or nothing to do with their appearance. This spiritual distortion is the result of narrowness of human vision, both their own and that of others. From this point he tries to determine the nature of the psychological ills, and in many cases their cause, in order to find the contributing factors that further their alienation from the main stream of life. He is interested in understanding and loving these twisted people, and he employs empathy, compassion, and intuition rather than analysis or fierce desire to cure.

In this first sketch, which delineates an old writer who has achieved an understanding of his fellow man and has retired from life to observe men and to teach them understanding, Anderson defines his problem symbolically by having the old writer say:

> . . . in the beginning when the world was young there were a great many thoughts but no such thing as a truth. Man made the truths himself and each truth was a composite of a great many vague thoughts. All about in the world were the truths and they were all beautiful. . . .

And then the people came along. Each as he appeared snatched up one of the truths and some who were quite strong snatched up a dozen of them.

It was the truths that made the people grotesques . . . the moment that one of the people took one of the truths to himself, called it his truth, and tried to live his life by it, he became a grotesque and the truth he embraced became a falsehood.

In the following stories in *Winesburg, Ohio* Anderson attempts to find in the lives of his people the contributing factors that have prevented them from reaching their full potential as human beings. He shows, too, his realization that the cause of man's distorted vision is not something as easily perceived and denounced as modern industrialism, but rather concepts that are as old as the human race— false ideas, false dreams, false hopes, and false goals. The indignities inflicted upon his people have made them spiritual grotesques, yet Anderson is attempting to see beyond their deformities and to know them.

Anderson's use of the word "grotesque" is quite important in this context. To him it does not connote revulsion or disgust; instead, he points out, the human grotesque is like the twisted and gnarled apples left behind in the orchards when the perfect fruit is picked. Small boys and the poor seek these apples eagerly because they know that the imperfect apples are the sweetest of all, perhaps even because of the surface blemishes that have caused them to be rejected. He also asserts that the spiritual ills of his people merely intensify their need for understanding and love.

After "The Book of the Grotesque," Anderson uses the first three stories to explore what he feels are the major aspects of the problem of human isolation. The first story, "Hands," deals with the inability to communicate feeling; the second, "Paper Pills," is devoted to the inability to communicate thought; and the third, "Mother," focuses on the inability to communicate love. According to Anderson, these three shortcomings are the real creators of the grotesques in human society, and these first three stories set the tone for the rest. Each of the three characters has encountered one aspect of the problem; he has something that he feels is vital and real within himself that he wants desperately to reveal to others. In each case he is rebuffed, and turning inward, he becomes a bit more worn and twisted spiritually. But, like the apples left in the orchards, he is the sweeter, the more human, for it. The revelation that he wants to communicate is in itself good; his inevitable tragedy lies in his inability to make it clear to others.

"Hands," the first of the stories, begins by describing the remarkably active and expressive hands of Wing Biddlebaum, an old recluse in the town. George Willard, a young reporter on the Winesburg *Eagle,* is fascinated by the old man's hands, and they become friends, seeking each other out and walking together through the streets. George knows intuitively that the man's hands are the secret to the man's isolation. He is curious to ask about them, and almost does; however, as Wing tells him that he must reject conformity, using his hands in his excitement, George becomes afraid; he no longer wants to knows the man's secret.

Anderson tells us: once as a schoolmaster in another town, Wing had been accused of making homosexual advances to his students because in his excitement he would touch them or tousle their hair. He fled, taking refuge in Winesburg. His hands had become a source of shame to him, and in Winesburg he tried to keep them hidden. In the town he is a pitiful and fearful creature, always expecting the spontaneous actions of his hands to be misinterpreted.

To Anderson, there are endless cases in which words either do not exist, or are rendered meaningless through overuse. Hence, the hands of a craftsman, a painter, a writer, a surgeon or a lover can communicate, without words, something of the truth and beauty that each feels inside. Even on a more mundane level, man's efforts to communicate with his fellows have often been dependent on his hands. But the language of hands is subject to misinterpretation, as is any other language. In the case of Wing Biddlebaum, the old man's words in the opening sketch are especially appropriate. Man himself asserts that homosexuality exists and is wrong; then, by misinterpreting the language of Wing's hands, he has distorted truth into falsehood, and has produced a grotesque. The reality behind the appearance of Wing's hands frightens young Willard. At this stage Willard is afraid to allow the friendship to deepen, because he senses that he, too, will be misunderstood.

In "Paper Pills" Anderson again writes of the relationship between a man's hands and his inner being, this time in the story of Doctor Reefy, a widower and a conventionally wise country general practitioner. Doctor Reefy is as cut off from effective communication with others as Wing Biddlebaum is in "Hands," his problem being his inability to communicate his thoughts without being misunderstood. Since he recognizes this shortcoming, he writes his thoughts on bits of paper and puts them into his pockets. There they become twisted into hard little balls, which he throws playfully at his friend the nurseryman.

Here Anderson further solidifies his comment that there is no such thing as truth, that there are only thoughts, and that man has made truths out of them through his own shortsightedness. Doctor Reefy knows that he is writing mere thoughts on the bits of paper, but he knows that they would be misinterpreted if he communicated them directly, so he lets them become a joke in the form of paper pills. He prefers that his paper pills be considered bits of paper and nothing more. In effect, the hard shells of the pills are the barriers of isolation that surround human minds. Voluntarily isolating himself instead of trying to overcome those barriers, he deliberately avoids inevitable misunderstanding.

This story has been interpreted by Waldo Frank[1] as representing the ineffectuality of isolated and fragmented human thought. However, Anderson indicates that there is no shortcoming in the thoughts themselves. Doctor Reefy had known love, beauty, and mystery, and been able to communicate these feelings to the girl whom he married; but he knew that words could not convey them to others. Rather than risk misinterpretation, he lets the paper pills be considered products of his gnarled hands rather than his heart. Even while he throws them playfully at his friend he hopes they will be seen as the expression of his soul. But the friend sees only the appearance, the work of Reefy's hands. Only understanding, intuitive or learned, can penetrate the hard shells of appearance. Reefy, knowing this is unlikely, lets himself become a grotesque because he cannot find the kind of understanding that he had shared briefly with his late wife.

The third story, "Mother," deals with the relationship between George Willard and his mother Elizabeth. The story explores a theme that Anderson had taken from his own experience and used in both *Windy McPherson's Son* and *Marching Men*: the inability to communicate love or understanding between mother and son. In the story, Elizabeth has been forced, because of her husband's business ineptitude, to take over management of both the family hotel and the family itself. She is resented by her husband as a usurper, and,

---

[1] Waldo Frank, " 'Winesburg, Ohio' After Twenty Years," *Story*, XIX (September–October 1944), 30.

unable to love or respect him, she focuses her interest and love on her son George. She sees the potential in George for the fulfillment she had been denied in a life spent in opposing both the forces of conventional success and her husband, with her son as the stake. Inwardly she violently defies anything that threatens her son; outwardly she is perfunctory, almost apologetic in his presence, hoping that he will understand her feelings and thereby give her life meaning.

Finally George announces that he is leaving home: "I just want to go away and look at people and think." She is unable to reply, but she knows that she has won. "She wanted to cry out with joy . . . but the expression of joy had become impossible to her," and the story ends in formality, the barriers still solid between mother and son.

In these three stories Anderson defines the problem of human isolation as it recurs in most of the other stories in *Winesburg, Ohio*. Something deep within each character demands expression. Unable to break through the shell that surrounds him, he turns in upon himself, becoming a grotesque, a person deserving of understanding and wanting it desperately, but completely unable to find it except in occasional instances, as in the embrace between Elizabeth and Doctor Reefy in "Death" and in the attempts made by many of the people of Winesburg in the following stories to seek understanding in George Willard. However, such moments of apparent understanding merely serve to emphasize the intensity of their isolation.

George Willard appears and reappears in about half of *Winesburg, Ohio* either as leading character, as an audience, or as a casual observer; his appearance thus gives a unity to the collection that makes it approach the novel form. More important, however, is his role in fully developing Anderson's theme. In two of the first three stories, "Hands" and "Mother," he plays the part ascribed to him in more than half of the following stories. To each of the grotesques, he appears to be what that individual wants him to be. To his mother he is an extension of herself through which her dreams may be fulfilled; to Wing Biddlebaum he is the symbol of the innocent love that had been denied him; to others he becomes, in turn, a symbol of a long-lost son, of father-confessor, of masculine strength and virility, of innocent, undemanding human understanding. His primary function to each one is that of an ear into which one can pour the inner stirrings of fear, hope, love, and dreams. Because his job as reporter on the Winesburg *Eagle* makes him part of the apparently integrated community, George Willard represents to the grotesques the line of communication and gives them opportunity to restore communication with the world from which each feels excluded. Because he is innocent, and unspoiled by the world that has rejected and isolated them, they feel they can talk to him.

In "The Philosopher," the story of Doctor Parcival, the role of George Willard as an ear into which the grotesque pours out his frustrations is especially obvious. Parcival often seeks out George in the *Eagle* office, and they talk, the doctor telling George fragments of stories out of his past. They were the things, the doctor said, that taught him to hate. But finally, after refusing a needless request to attend a dead child, in fear of his life, the doctor lets his mask of hate slip, and he tells George his belief: his compassion for man and his inability to save him have convinced him that ". . . Everyone in the world is Christ and they are all crucified."

However, "Nobody Knows" demonstrates that George at this stage, like the society of which he is a part, does not understand the grotesque's attempt at communication. After receiving a note from Louise Trunnion seeking him out for a moment of love, he meets her secretly, and they make love without realizing the emptiness of the act. The sex act and the overtures preceding it were a fumbling search for understanding on the part of Louise that is misinterpreted by George, and he is unsatisfied and afraid as a result.

"Godliness," a four-part tale, is the most complex of the stories. One of those in which George Willard does not appear, it incorporates more than three generations on an Ohio farm. In it Anderson shows the passing of pioneer innocence and the rise of materialism. In the story Jesse Bentley, the family patriarch, is dominated by the Calvinistic interpretation of God's favor being manifested in material wealth; as he grows richer he becomes convinced that he is God's chosen instrument to work His will. Finally, as he frightens his grandson with his Biblical fervor, he begins to doubt. His daughter, seeking the love that she cannot find from her father, takes a lover, and eventually she marries in confusion. In the end the old man frightens the boy again with an Old Testament-inspired sacrifice designed to alleviate his doubts, and the boy strikes his grandfather with a stone and runs off into the unknown.

In "Godliness," Anderson uses theme as well as setting to tie the story into the book. In this instance, the theme of isolation stems not from human shortcomings alone but also from the new false god of materialism, a god that depends for its success upon the continued isolation of human beings. Jesse Bentley is made grotesque and frightening; his daughter is denied love and understanding; and his grandson is driven away in terror. They are all unable to find release from the service of the puritan and materialistic god the old man has erected. For the daughter and her son, Anderson shows his compassion and love; he has none for the old man completely dominated by his false god.

In "A Man of Ideas," Anderson shows Joe Welling's ludicrous and futile efforts to break the barriers surrounding him until his love for a lean, tired woman gives him hope. But Alice Hindman, of "Adventure," finds nothing. Desperately wanting to love another lost being like herself, she runs naked into the rain, humiliates herself, and finally realizes that she, like so many others, must live and die alone in Winesburg.

Wash Williams in "Respectability" is both physically and psychologically grotesque, despite which, his well-cared-for hands had once made him the best telegrapher in the state. In an intense moment prompted by George Willard's idle questioning he pours out his story: his mother-in-law had once attempted to effect a reconciliation between him and his unfaithful wife by conspiring to make him see her naked. But her love affairs had destroyed the love he once felt; as a result of his mother-in-law's trick he began to hate women and became twisted into the grim figure that Winesburg knows.

"The Thinker" shows Seth Richmond's inability to communicate his hunger for life to his mother, to Helen White, the banker's daughter, whom he sees as a symbol of purity and innocence, or to his friend George Willard. Sick of the idle, meaningless talk to which he appears doomed, and fearing that Helen will eventually marry the articulate George, Seth turns on Willard furiously because George seems to have the ability to communicate with others that he lacks. But the following sketch, "Tandy," indicates that the vision of wholeness and of perfect understanding may be communicated to a recipient who is innocent and unspoiled.

The two most closely interwoven narratives in *Winesburg, Ohio* are "The Strength of God" and "The Teacher," in both of which a minister and a schoolteacher interpret their personal loneliness and need for love as sin. George Willard, in his roles as an observer in "The Strength of God" and a catalyst in "The Teacher," begins to

realize that there is a truth about human life that he is missing.
For George it is the beginning of wisdom.

In "The Strength of God" the devout Presbyterian minister,
Reverend Hartman, suddenly discovers that he is a peeping tom,
spying on Kate Swift, the schoolteacher, in her room. Convinced
that he is damned, he continues compulsively until the sight of
Kate praying in anguish reverses his conviction, and he startles
George Willard by proclaiming that he has been saved by a vision
of her. In this instance, the minister's need for human understanding
has been distorted to a renewal of a perverted faith by fright and
a neurotic conviction of sin.

The second story reveals the source of Kate Swift's anguish. She
had been George Willard's teacher and had continued to advise him
until one night in her fervor, she had taken him in her arms. Frightened by her actions, she ran home to pray, the result being the
sight the minister had seen. However, due to the growth of his
intuitive wisdom, George realizes that it is not sex she is seeking;
instead, he is confused as he leaves her, and tells himself, "I have
missed something. I have missed something Kate Swift was trying
to tell me." But Kate has no means of telling George or anyone
else what it is that she is seeking.

"Loneliness" describes a twofold manifestation of human isolation
so severe that it drives Enoch Robinson into the supposed security
of a single room and then denies him even that security. An artist
who had returned to Winesburg after an unsuccessful marriage,
Robinson tells George of the peculiar isolation of the artist in a
society that makes special demands on him while it denies understanding until finally he flees, driven from his work and losing the
only means whereby he can reveal his dream. Robinson's isolation
is not only that of other men; it is also the peculiar isolation that
only the unfulfilled artist can know.

The story of Belle Carpenter in "An Awakening" leads George
Willard further along the road to eventual understanding of his
fellows; at the same time, it gives him further insight into the
forces of misunderstanding that drive them into isolation. Belle and
George are friends; George seeks her out one night to tell her of
his growing insight into life. But in a moment of excitement he
takes her in his arms, and the inarticulate bartender who had been
pursuing Belle jumps out of the bushes and assaults George. Slinking
home in bewilderment, George does not comprehend that for a

moment he had been close to breaking the bonds of isolation, but
thinks that he had allowed himself to be tricked into thinking that
the power he felt was sexual rather than the force of insight.

In "Queer," the story of Elmer Cowley, one of the grotesques
again assaults George Willard. Just as the others see George as the
symbol of liberation, Elmer sees George as a manifestation of the
society that rejects him. But although he resents George, he attempts
to become friendly with him. Failing this, he strikes George, leaving
him bewildered and half-conscious. As he jumps on a freight train
to leave Winesburg, Elmer voices his frustration by crying, "I guess
I showed him. I ain't so queer. I guess I showed him I ain't so
queer."

In this story Elmer Cowley points out what most of the other
grotesques have failed to perceive: George Willard does not understand them. The others believe that he does; even when he leaves
each of them in bewilderment, the grotesques completely misunder-
stand his sympathy. Although he is still too young and inexperienced
to perceive what they try to tell him, his contacts with them are
teaching him compassion and empathy, qualities that will in time
permit him to know and understand others. Moreover, each of their
revelations contributes to his spiritual growth.

After "Queer," Anderson turns to the Clyde countryside for the
setting of "The Untold Lie," using as his theme the difficulty of
understanding, much less communicating, the ambiguous meaning of
experience. In this case, Hal Winters, a married farm hand, is unable to give his young friend advice about marriage. Seeing it to
be a meaningless trap, and yet realizing it has moments of closeness, he turns away in the dark, unable to know a definable truth.

In "Drink," Willard learns for himself the ambiguous nature of
experience and the attendant difficulties it presents. Tom Foster is
an outsider, both by birth and by nature. He is too innocent to be
condemned merely because he is at once possessed by an impossible
dream of understanding. But George, schooled by experience, condemns Foster's drunken dreams of Helen White, whom Tom, like
Seth Richmond in "The Thinker," loves for her innocence and
purity; nevertheless, George is drawn to the boy who wants to
experience everything—except hurting others.

At this point, George Willard's education is almost complete;
there is nothing more that the people of Winesburg can teach him,
now he must go into the world and learn for himself. In "Death,"

the means of release are provided by his mother's death, which breaks the tie that has held him. At the same time it is revealed that she and Doctor Reefy had known and loved each other because they had shared moments of understanding. George, however, does not know this; he is overwhelmed by his sudden knowledge of the ultimate isolation of death.

"Sophistication" provides the final lesson that leads George into complete manhood. In his first and last quiet encounter with Helen White, the girl he has loved from afar, George now sees her as Seth Richmond and Tom Foster have seen her, as a symbol of spiritual fulfillment rather than as an object of physical love. He realizes that a moment of shared understanding transcends anything that might be found in a physical union. Based on his new insight he senses that pure love, even when uncomplicated by society's imposed pressures or its misguided interpretations, can easily lead to misinterpretation and isolation. For a moment, however, each of them had come close to knowing and understanding the other.

In these last two stories Anderson comes close to formulating a tentative solution to the problem of human isolation. He feels that it can only be overcome when human beings meet under circumstances that forbid the entrance of the thoughts that had become social truth and therefore have no validity, save to warp and distort the human soul. As the old writer in the opening sketch had observed, this is the cause of man's grotesqueness. George Willard has learned that this distortion can only be cured by searching out moments of compassion, of empathy, of love. Anderson indicates that George has passed from an attitude of detached curiosity to a search for understanding. Having learned something of the nature of the human heart, he has learned to listen with his own heart rather than with ears that have become too accustomed to the sound of the "truths become falsehoods" all around him.

After the final revelation in "Sophistication," the episode of "Departure" is anticlimactic for George. In the microcosm of human nature that is Winesburg he has learned the fundamental secret of human life: that one must reach out and accept and love; he has ". . . for a moment taken hold of the one thing that makes the mature life of men and women in the modern world possible"; and he is ready to assume his place in that world. As he leaves Winesburg he takes with him something of each of the grotesques who sought him out, and he knows that he can find understanding and fulfillment only in moments of uncomplicated acceptance and love.

Willard's role is the means through which thematic development becomes apparent in *Winesburg, Ohio*. Human isolation can be overcome and man can achieve an understanding relationship with his fellows, Anderson asserts, only through intuitive perception. The normal processes of direct communication are useless; what is needed are deliberate efforts to attain empathy through compassion, through love, and above all, through intuition. Anderson shows that this lesson can be learned through the evolution of Willard's experience from complete misunderstanding through increasing awareness and finally into a state where understanding and fulfillment become possible, at least momentarily.

However, *Winesburg, Ohio* is not merely an exposition of human isolation, nor is it a story of adult initiation; in the last analysis, it is about people, and George Willard is secondary in importance to the individual on whom each story centers. *Winesburg, Ohio* is Anderson's affirmation of his belief in the durability of the human spirit and his assertion that the compassion he feels is necessary for meaningful human relations. He points out that all men share the common bond of humanity, and they must recognize this kinship and avoid its distortions if they are to survive.

Winesburg, Ohio also provides a vivid glimpse of the late nineteenth-century American town poised between continuing handicraftsmanship and industrialism. Anderson shows the closeness of nature, a nature that the townspeople either take for granted or ignore; but the presence of the creek, the trees, the frost, the sky, and the sweeping flat countryside of northwest Ohio prevents them from effectively denying their origins. The town itself is graphically portrayed, from the high board fence covered with colorful circus posters to the grimy brick walls of the alley behind the office of the Winesburg *Eagle,* from the weekly stillness of the country lanes to the air of excitement on Main Street on Saturday night. Lining the streets are the houses, solid and enduring; however, a board exterior often covers a structure of logs. Not only is the pioneer past only a generation away in time, but the briefness of man's tenure in Winesburg contrasts sharply with the imperviousness of the impersonal walls he has erected.

Although Anderson's people are highly individualized in their microcosmic setting, characterization is not fully developed. Instead, each person is primarily defined by a controlling characteristic that provides both the key to his individuality and the nature of his grotesqueness. This method of characterization is also a unifying factor in the work, for Anderson joins the stories in which George Willard does not appear to the others in the book by utilizing not only the same background and theme but also the same technique: a revealing moment in which the reader is permitted to grasp the nature of someone's isolation and the controlling characteristic of his individuality. But that the essence of each of the characters can be revealed in a phrase or an incident does not mean that characterizations in the stories are slight or simple; rather, they are achieved through depth rather than breadth; each is a narrow area deeply explored.

This concept of characterization leads to the narrative technique that Anderson has employed in the stories. They are character-plotted, and the action reveals the essence of the central figure's being. Outside events in the stories are normally of little or no importance except as they provide opportunity for this revelation. In effect, Anderson has primarily been providing opportunity for his reader to peer deeply into a man's soul. In each story this intimate revelation is made quickly, sometimes in a phrase, a sentence, or a paragraph, but in each one Anderson has revealed, with compassion, the deepest secret of each character's being.

In attempting to measure the achievement of *Winesburg, Ohio,* critics have evolved numerous conflicting theories. In the 1920s it was called naturalistic or realistic; in the 1930s it was primitivistic; and more recently critics have seen in it an elaborate structure designed to construct a new myth of the American small town. The continued attention still given to the volume indicates the respect in which it is held, and the controversy it can still arouse. However, Anderson is not expounding the theory of a universe of mechanistic forces operating on his people, as naturalism implies; he is showing the essence of their humanity. Neither does he depend for effect upon the constant and careful accumulation of sharply drawn, realistic detail; rather he sketches, he implies, he insinuates. He uses insight based on introspection in order to arrive at delineation of character and of situation. Neither naturalism nor realism is satisfactory as a descriptive term because the stories cannot be twisted or distorted to meet the demands of their meanings. Those who term it primitivistic attempt to categorize by subject matter, ignoring what Anderson was trying to say.

The interpretation of the work as an attempt to construct an elaborate American myth is an unnecessary complication that never occurred to Anderson. He was not writing about society, either realistically or in a symbolic myth; he was writing about people, each of whom is conceived and presented as an individual rather than merely another manifestation of society. That that person is part of the social structure is important only insofar as every individual is part of society, and Anderson was not merely interested in treating the individual in terms of that relationship; he was interested in treating the individual as a human being. Thus, George Willard, whose role as reporter might be considered a symbolic one, never writes a news story in the book.

Winesburg, Ohio is the book that provides the solid foundation of Anderson's literary reputation, and his accomplishment in the work is impressive. It is not a book of rebellion, as were his earlier works of fiction; instead, it is an affirmation of his belief in the durability of the human spirit and of the compassion that he felt was needed among men. In it Anderson has examined the problem of human isolation, not in the hope of curing it, but in the certainty of his belief that man himself is important individually rather than collectively.

By examining so many specific instances of human isolation, Anderson shows a far greater understanding of the nature of the problem than he had in his two earlier novels. This major shift in approach indicates that he was consciously avoiding the earlier mistake of oversimplification. His most important discovery, however, was his realization that human isolation stems entirely from human shortcomings; those inherent in sex, in inarticulateness, in ". . . the old brutal ignorance that had in it also a kind of beautiful childlike innocence . . . ," and even in deliberate cruelty. Occasionally, however, when he perceived that the new materialism was making inroads among his people, as in "Godliness" and in "Queer," and the central figures were isolated by greed, flashes of the old Anderson shine through. For the greedy ones he had contempt, and he replaces compassion and hope with irony, which at times, as in "Queer," becomes bitter.

Winesburg, Ohio is not an isolated achievement, standing apart from Anderson's earlier works. Although as literary art it is far superior to his other works, the thematic structure of *Winesburg* is actually an intensification of that in *Windy McPherson's Son* and

Marching Men. Equally obvious are stylistic and structural relationships. In *Winesburg,* the rhetorical awkwardness apparent in *Windy McPherson's Son,* has almost disappeared; however, this writing fault had been less conspicuous in *Marching Men* and was less evident in *Mid-American Chants.* Conversely the experimentation with the natural rhythms of American speech that he had conducted in *Mid-American Chants* has in *Winesburg* become his major stylistic characteristic, pointing toward his mastery of the reproduction of the oral storytelling tradition that halts, digresses, becomes seemingly irrelevant at times, and yet proceeds swiftly toward a carefully defined climax and impact. Conversations have become almost entirely natural; the flat, naturally reproduced, Midwestern tones replacing the earlier imitative and artificial rhetorical flourishes. Characterization, in contrast to the earlier surface treatment, has deepened and the storytelling technique has become carefully controlled and orderly. Throughout the book and in most of the individual stories there is evidence of an artistic plan. In *Winesburg, Ohio* Anderson knew where he was going, and he was aware of the implications of his theme. Each of the stories is a manifestation of that theme, and through the regular appearance of George Willard, the solution to the problem of human isolation becomes increasingly evident as George approaches eventual understanding.

To strengthen the book's structure and to document his thesis, Anderson starts and ends the volume with a sketch. "The Book of the Grotesque" sets up the problem of human isolation and presents its origins in symbolic terms; "Departure" shows that these shortcomings, made real in the stories, are not insurmountable, that there is hope if the individual seeks out the basis of understanding among men.

With the publication of *Winesburg, Ohio* Anderson had achieved full stature as a writer, a stature, however, that could not remain static. Rather, the book marks both the end of the earliest period in his writing career and the beginning of the second. It represents the culmination of his discovery of his own particular talents and his own view of individual lives; it also points out the directions that his future works were to take: two directions that are diametrically opposed, one of them looking backward in time at the American past and the other looking forward into the age of industrialism that had once been his prime interest.

Winesburg, Ohio, in its re-creation of the past, with which Ander-

son was to become increasingly concerned both in later works and
in his own life, is permeated with an air of nostalgia; a wished-for
return to a state of human society that was uncomplicated. But
Anderson realized that the past is not perfect, nor did he want it
so. He recognized ". . . the fact that many people must live and
die alone, even in Winesburg." However, he believed that understanding could more easily be achieved in a world less complicated
and less dehumanized than the age of industrialism. In this sense
the book nostalgically evokes the memory of a way of life that is
gone, as is evident in the description of George Willard's departure.
As George looks back, he notes that ". . . the town of Winesburg
had disappeared, and his life there had become but a background
upon which to paint the dreams of his manhood."

When *Winesburg, Ohio* was published, Anderson was already at
work on a novel designed to carry Winesburg and its people into
the new age of industrialism; he was broadening his personal contacts with that age and he was moving confidently into what he felt
was the main stream of intellectual and artistic life in the America
of his time. The Chicago liberation had served its purpose and had
almost run its course; he had a solid literary achievement behind
him; he felt that he could break ties with advertising and fully
realize the literary success and personal fulfillment he had earned.

Winesburg, Ohio, he believed, had been a beginning for him, an
exercise in understanding that would permit him to move forward,
examining increasingly large areas of the American experience, and
eventually to achieve what the fictionalized versions of himself in
the novels had sought. But, in spite of his success in *Winesburg,
Ohio,* he had yet to understand the peculiar nature of his own
literary gift, and he still did not realize the enormity and complexity of the experience that he was trying to assimilate, understand, and define.

4

SOCIAL ANALYSIS AND DESPAIR

I N spite of Anderson's realization that *Winesburg, Ohio* was a
substantial literary work, he was generally unhappy and dis-
satisfied with his life. He hated advertising; he was disenchanted
with the Chicago renaissance; and he knew that *Winesburg, Ohio*
was just a beginning. He wrote to Trigant Burrow ". . . it seems
to me that I am now ripe to do something, and I hate to see the
years and days go by in the writing of advertisements for somebody's canned tomatoes. . . ." [1]

People were willing to pay him for writing nonsense but not for
writing what he believed. He went to New York and tried writing
motion picture publicity while he worked on a new novel, *Poor
White,* but returned to Chicago in disgust. Chicago was no better;
even the literary movement had degenerated, he felt. To his new
friend, Van Wyck Brooks, he revealed the source of his dissatisfaction:

> One has to realize that, although there is truth in the Winesburg
> things, there is another big story to be done. We are no longer the
> old America. Those are tales of farming people. We've got a new
> people now. We are a growing, shifting, changing thing. Our life in
> our factory towns intensifies. It becomes at the same time more ugly
> and more intense.
>
> God damn it, Brooks, I wish my books would sell for one reason.
> I want to quit working for a living and go wander for five years in
> our towns. I want to be a factory hand again and wander from place
> to place. I want my frame to unbend from the desk and to go back
> and listen to this new thing.

During 1918 and 1919 Anderson spent as much time as he could
away from Chicago, advertising, and from his second wife, Tennes-

---

[1] Sherwood Anderson, *Letters of Sherwood Anderson,* eds. Howard Mumford
Jones and Walter P. Rideout (Boston, 1953), p. 45. Unless otherwise cited,
all letters quoted are from this source.

see. In many respects it was Elyria all over again. He had to make a break. An attack of influenza in January, 1920, gave him a chance to leave Chicago and go to Mobile, Alabama, to recuperate. There he finished *Poor White,* and returned to Chicago temporarily refreshed. "Back here," he wrote, "I almost feel able to say I don't care if I never travel again. The place between mountain and mountain I call Mid-America is my land. Good or bad, it's all I'll ever have."

Poor White was published shortly after his return to Chicago. He felt that in it he had built on the *Winesburg, Ohio* accomplishment as he carried the people of Winesburg into the new age of industrialism that had begun its domination of the Midwest. As Anderson remarked in the introduction to the Modern Library edition of the novel, it was in that sense the biography of a town during its transition from an agricultural to an industrial economy. Anderson's statement must not be taken literally, however, because he knew that he must focus on individuals. *Poor White* is not the biography of a town; it is the biography of the people in the town whose lives have been warped by industrialism and its concomitant, greed. He focuses on fewer people, but in more detail, essentially attempting to employ the same technique that he had used so successfully in *Winesburg.*

The scope of the novel is as broad as the history of the Midwest. In going back in time to attempt to identify the origins of the Midwestern experience, Anderson draws on the work of a fellow Midwesterner, Mark Twain, whom he held in deep admiration. He begins *Poor White* in the area that is Mark Twain's America—the Mississippi—and in the age of innocence and brutality that produced *Huckleberry Finn.* Out of this environment Anderson brings Hugh McVey, who becomes for Anderson the unwitting symbol of man in the new age.

McVey's father is a drunkard, and in Hugh's early years in Mudcat Landing, Missouri, Anderson shows the first evidence of the loss of innocence and the intensification of brutality. The coming of the railroad provides the means whereby McVey enters the new age. Employed at the new railroad station, the stationmaster's New Englander wife "civilizes" him as the Widow Douglas had attempted to civilize Huck Finn. Accepting her philosophy that it is sinful to dream or to idle along the river, McVey becomes determined to succeed in the world.

Here Anderson touches upon a phenomenon noted by other Mid-western novelists: the impact on the area of New England Puritanism, with its emphasis on hard work and material gain as the meaningful elements of life. It is interesting to note that Louis Bromfield later called this pragmatic, materialistic philosophy the influence of the peddler. Clyde, Ohio, on the edge of New England's Western Reserve, had given Anderson the opportunity to see it in action.

In spite of his day-dreaming tendency, McVey becomes a skilled telegrapher, practicing his trade throughout the Midwest, in time coming to Bidwell, Ohio. As Anderson describes the town and the time, it is Winesburg as it was when George Willard left it:

. . . every one knew his neighbor and was known to him. Strangers did not come and go swiftly and mysteriously and there was no constant and confusing roar of machinery and new projects underfoot. For the moment mankind seemed about to take time to try to understand itself.

But Bidwell was poised on the verge of the new age, and a wise man of the town who saw the change coming commented: "Well, there's going to be a new war here. . . . It won't be like the Civil War, just shooting off guns and killing people's bodies. At first it's going to be a war to see to what class a man must belong; then it's going to be a long, silent war between classes, between those who have and those who can't get. It'll be the worst war of all."

Hugh McVey, the unknowing instrument of the age, is to precipitate that war. He becomes an inventor, his inventions are recognized by the young men of affairs in the town, and in time, Bidwell becomes an industrial center. However, McVey remains convinced that his inventions will make life easy, will bring men together, and destroy the old brutalities that he had seen in his wandering. Therefore, when he sees his dreams of peace replaced by the realities of greed, corruption, and cruelty, brought about by the town's new industrialism, he is horrified at what he has done. Too late, McVey rebels, the war prophesied by the old man comes true, and Bidwell reaps a harvest of oppression, indignity, and violence. McVey, like Anderson's earlier heroes, can only turn his back on the industrial giant and seek meaning elsewhere.

In focusing on Hugh McVey, Anderson clearly shows the new industrialism's impact on the individual, and by extension, on every level of society, from the country squire-turned entrepreneur to the farm boy-turned millhand. In each case, industrialism results in an intensified isolation, an often confused and meaningless sense of values, and a pronounced and deliberate inhumanity.

Hugh McVey is more than a character study; however, he is also Anderson's attempt to embody the essence of the American myth as it has been taken over by materialism. To accomplish this feat, Anderson uses both Thomas Edison and Abraham Lincoln as models for the adult Hugh McVey. Like Edison, McVey can see straight to the heart of a practical problem and solve it, making life more convenient and becoming rich in the process. But Anderson gives McVey an insight into human worth that a practical man rarely has time for, and the combination produces a man who is to industrialism what Lincoln was to political affairs.

Utilizing physical awkwardness, a dreamy nature, a sense of isolation, as well as practicality and compassion, Anderson has carefully constructed the similarity between McVey and Lincoln, making McVey the Lincoln of industrialism. Anderson has done this because he has seen the parallel between the struggle of which Lincoln became the central figure and that which he intends to symbolize by McVey. Lincoln's struggle was to advance political freedom, an advance that would, in time, result in spiritual freedom and the ennobling of man. Anderson portrays McVey's struggle as an attempt to free man from drudgery through his inventions.

McVey's origins, like Lincoln's, are humble and obscure, firmly rooted in the frontier traditions of personal freedom and individualism. At the same time, each transcends the ruggedness of frontier individualism through his belief that human compassion makes him his brother's keeper rather than his competitor. In each, dreamy idealism and practical dedication clash to bring about a stormy balance. Being both taciturn and unpretentious, each has determined to meet the problem of human liberation head on, seeking an idealistic solution in a practical way. Finally, each sees his goal almost within reach.

However, because of their dichotomous natures, each has become an unwitting tool, both of men whose motives are less noble than their own and of social and economic forces of the age. They lose control of the forces they had been instrumental in unleashing, the result being a new and more vicious enslavement. Lincoln's death left these forces unleashed, resulting in the chaos of Reconstruction, but Anderson has McVey live, and McVey's knowledge of what industrialism has done and his resolution to find a cure for its evils, leave hope for the future.

McVey does not use the Machiavellian concept of the ends justifying the means as another well-paid servant of industrialism might do. His innate sense of honesty revolts at the theft of another man's patents. He will not even allow his wife, the daughter of the richest man in Bidwell, to aid him financially. Before her marriage she had revolted against the forces of convention that threatened to make her a grotesque, and throughout the novel she continues to rebel against industrialism and materialism. She is the embodiment of the free spirit who refuses to let herself become imprisoned and distorted. In spite of the misunderstandings that inevitably result from her behavior, she maintains her personal integrity and tries to expand it through intimacy with others. She teaches McVey that he, too, can be a free spirit, and as his search for fulfillment begins, he knows that her way rather than industrialism and rampant materialism will lead to ultimate success. McVey and his wife, therefore, carry out the dictum that Anderson had proposed in *Winesburg, Ohio*: to ignore the surface of human life and to probe intuitively and compassionately beneath it for a common understanding that rejects the arbitrary barriers of master and servant, husband and wife, and makes possible mature love between two human beings.

On lower social levels the impact of industrialism is brutal and overwhelming. In scenes reminiscent of the moments of insight in *Winesburg, Ohio*, Anderson shows the farm hand who comes to the factory to escape the isolated drudgery of the farm, only to find a more intense isolation, and more degrading job in the factory; he portrays the bewilderment of Joe Wainsworth, the harness maker, whose craft has been superseded by the machines; he shows the complete degeneration of the townspeople from human to materialistic values as they search for fulfillment through the acceptance of the new age.

As Anderson sees it, the struggle in Bidwell is the attempt to find and retain human values in the face of a whistling, screeching, triumphant industrialism. He had faced a similar problem in *Windy McPherson's Son* and *Marching Men*, but *Poor White* marks an advance in Anderson's approach to the problem. Industrialism is no longer the source of human ills, as Anderson had maintained in the two earlier novels. Anderson now sees industrialism as a potential source of good, but when it is dominated by greed it becomes evil. These townspeople, warped by their contact with industrialism, now exhibit a brutality that is deliberate and intensified. In spite of the inherent mockery of the triumphant whistles in the background, Anderson concludes *Poor White* with the hope that man may in time regain his innocence and reassert his human values. But until then, he can see only tragedy for the farm hands, the harness makers, and the poor whites.

Poor White, although a complex and important work that is one of Anderson's best, is marred by problems of structure as was *Windy McPherson's Son* and *Marching Men.* However, the artificiality of style, diction, and conversation in the earlier novels is replaced by the natural idioms and rhythms of *Winesburg, Ohio.* His use of digressions, important parts of his storytelling technique in the stories of *Winesburg,* hinder the narrative flow in *Poor White.* Moreover, the optimistic but indecisive ending indicates that Anderson had not yet learned how to end a novel. Indecision is acceptable at the end of a short story or a sketch, which represents only part of life, but in a novel, it indicates a much larger story that has not been told.

In the short stories these shortcomings are strengths when they are combined with Anderson's ability to penetrate the character's essence, but in his novels they indicate that Anderson's narrative ability lies in his propensity to tell only part of a story. In the short stories the reader feels that he has been permitted a brief, but revealing, glimpse beneath the surface of life; in the novels he has much more than a glimpse, but he is no closer to the ultimate meaning of life. In *Poor White,* the individual sketches remain vivid, but the expository writing necessary to a novel is weak and detracts from the novel's effectiveness. Nevertheless Anderson's fusion of subject matter, style, and theme makes it a major achievement.

The reception of *Poor White* was good, but sales were light, and Anderson's future seemed tied to advertising. He worked sporadically on free verse, on a never completed novel, and on stories in the *Winesburg* style. At the same time, poison-pen letters began to accuse him of writing filth in *Winesburg, Ohio.* Even friends misinterpreted the book; to Van Wyck Brooks he wrote, "It did hurt . . . when I found you also taking *Winesburg* . . . as a sex book." In the *Memoirs* he recalls that "At the time I was half ill for months. 'I will write no more,' I told myself, and sometimes when

I had received . . . perhaps a half dozen abusive letters I went and got drunk. 'If I am so filthy I shall be filthy' I told myself."

He abandoned the verse and the unfinished novel in favor of sustained work on the short stories and sketches for *The Triumph of the Egg*, which he began to see as a unified collection, looser than the *Winesburg* group, but unified in theme. At this point he wrote the grim "Out of Nowhere into Nothing," completing the collection. At loose ends then, he was casting about when Paul Rosenfeld offered to pay passage to Europe for both him and Tennessee. He accepted immediately, and in May 1921, he and Tennessee sailed for a three-month visit.

James Schevill attributes the abrupt change in Anderson's handling of sex[2] to this visit. In the earlier works, the sex act is either a brutal hunger or a furtive, mutually unsatisfactory relationship; but in later works he tries to bring it into the open so that it may be seen as healthy and good. Schevill's statement may be an over-simplification, but in the notebook that Anderson kept during the trip he recorded his admiration for the frankness with which the French regarded the human body and sexual love.

On his return from Europe, Anderson's fortunes improved. In October 1921, he was awarded the *Dial* magazine prize of $2000 for a promising writer. Anderson, at 45, accepted gratefully, and the ensuing publicity increased demand for his earlier books. When *The Triumph of the Egg* appeared that fall and was well received, Anderson saw the chance to break with advertising and the dying Chicago group, and to end his marriage to Tennessee. Again, as in Elyria, his break had to be complete.

The Triumph of the Egg is a major achievement. Unlike *Winesburg, Ohio*, it is not unified in character, setting, and time, but it does contain a consistent thematic statement of Anderson's view, at that time, of the ultimate end of human life. Once again he focuses upon the lives of people who have become grotesques, with the exception that there is no George Willard to grow in understanding. Consequently, the intensity of Anderson's premise that there is no hope for these people accumulates, and the book culminates in despair. In all of Anderson's preceding works, in spite of the personal tragedies that occur, he had ended on a note suggesting the possibility that personal fulfillment may ultimately be

[2] James Schevill, *Sherwood Anderson: His Life and Works,* (Denver: University of Denver press, 1951), p. 139.

attained; in *The Triumph of the Egg* that possibility does not exist.

For structural unity Anderson begins and ends the collection with a brief prose poem, the first of which, "The Dumb Man," sets forth the theme of the book. In it, in the midst of an apparently meaningless incident, Anderson points out that even if love, understanding, and fulfillment are found, they cannot be communicated to others. "I have a wonderful story to tell but know no way of telling it," he laments in despair.

As in *Winesburg, Ohio*, Anderson is primarily concerned with the problem of human isolation in each of the stories in *The Triumph of the Egg*; but the feeling of inadequacy, frustration, and despair emanating from "The Dumb Man" finds its way, unmitigatedly, into the human lives and relationships that are being investigated. Anderson in his intuitive grasp of the essence of each life, also uncovers the tragic inadequacy in each.

In the first story, "I Want to Know Why," Anderson returns to the Midwest and to a boy's initial awareness of the imponderable realities of life. Widely anthologized, the story is often considered a classic example of the theme of an adolescent's initiation. But when the story is read in the context of Anderson's work, and in its position in this volume following the initial declaration of frustration and despair, it takes on a more significant meaning. "I Want to Know Why" is Anderson's expression of the most important of adult tragedies: the inability to understand the complexity of emotions and the confusion of values evident not only in society, but in each individual human being. Anderson's adolescent narrator is still young enough to give voice to the resulting frustration, a frustration that the adult would be expected to accept.

The boy's life is dominated by his fondness for race horses. He follows the races to a meet at Saratoga. In the course of the story, Anderson examines the values of society and of individuals through the eyes of the boy, noting the contradictions and the illogicalities inherent in life; at the end the boy protests his inability to understand them. The first of these contradictions is simple: a white man will tell on a bad or mischievous boy; a Negro man won't. The boy makes no attempt to explain the contradiction, but he muses on it; meanwhile Anderson implies that the white men, having given their allegiance to a standard of values outside themselves, have lost their ability to understand. The Negroes, on the other hand, have not had to make that concession, and their understanding remains intimate and uncomplicated.

Other contradictions become apparent to the boy: the good, generous man who is condemned because he is a gambler; the men who fail to see the beauty of a race horse but see him only as a vehicle for gambling. (The Negroes, however, can see and appreciate that beauty, but few white adults can.) The most important contradiction is that which gives rise to the title: how can the trainer of a beautiful, smoothly coordinated race horse visit a prostitute who, while superficially attractive, ". . . is not clean . . . but with a hard, ugly mouth"? Here is a man who has seen real beauty, yet he refuses to recognize it and turns instead to a cheap substitute. Man's basic confusion of values is his inability to distinguish between appearance and reality, and the boy, like Anderson, is unable to explain it.

In this instance, Anderson is not talking about an adolescent's initiation to life; he is protesting the same confusion of values that had misled Sam McPherson and Hugh McVey. In this story, however, Anderson acknowledges that the problem is too deeply rooted in natural drives as well as society's standards to be resolved either by personal rebellion or rejection or by sudden altruism. Man at this point seems incapable of distinguishing between the beautiful and the tawdry, the real and the make-believe.

Critics have commented adversely on the lapses in style that permit occasional glimpses of the adult narrator who has intruded on the boy's story. However, these are conscious, artistic lapses; like Jonathan Swift, Anderson adopts a mask, which he lets slip when he wants to minimize misinterpretation. The boy is confused at the dichotomy of values that has destroyed his world; the adult despairs because he can do nothing about it.

In the second story, "Seeds," Anderson makes another comment on man's inability to understand beauty and love. The story opens with a dialogue between an artist and a psychoanalyst, and it concludes with a sketch. In the dialogue, Anderson derides the scientific approach: "It is given to no man to venture far along the road of human lives. . . . Fool—do you expect love to be understood?" Only the artist, with compassion and understanding, can penetrate the dead thoughts that choke living men. The sketch depicts the tragedy of a young woman who confuses sex with love.

We know that love will save us, Anderson concludes, but we are unable to recognize it.

"The Egg" is the most complex story in the collection. On the surface it is the story of another grotesque, a man who is incapable of being an accepted success of the sort that he and society respect. His comic efforts to give the public what he thinks it wants only make him ridiculous and compound his frustration. Again Anderson uses an adolescent narrator who sympathizes with his father, but, like the boy in "I Want to Know Why," he can do nothing but speculate on the causes of his father's despair.

At the same time, the boy is unable to laugh at his father's ridiculous attempts, as Anderson is unable to convey laughter in this or in any other of the seemingly humorous stories in the collection. He knows that the custard pie in the face is an affront to the dignity of the man who receives it. Therefore, in "The Egg," he is probing beneath the seemingly humorous and ridiculous to know the man as a grotesque, who is the sweeter and the more human for his grotesqueness.

Within this sympathetic portrayal of a grotesque, Anderson includes a symbolic level that illustrates the frustration he feels at his inability to understand through intuition the source and meaning of man's tragedy. In nature the problem of deformity is easily solved. If an egg produces a chicken that is physically grotesque, the monster dies; however, a human father will attempt to preserve the life of what is symbolically his image. Albeit, man's most serious deformity is spiritual, and it is not fatal; he lives, but because he is grotesque he is prevented from attaining fulfillment. The egg contains the secret of life; but just as that secret is hidden by a strong but fragile shell, so is the secret of man's grotesqueness and tragedy hidden by appearance. When attempts are made to penetrate the shell, it explodes. If man persists in his efforts to find the secret of human life, not only is he defeated, but he makes a fool of himself; as Anderson stated in "Seeds," man is not permitted "to venture far along the road of human lives." The egg, in the end, retains its secret inviolate, its triumph complete.

The father in the story is significant as a contrast to the father portrayals in Anderson's earlier works. For the first time Anderson shows that because the father is a grotesque, he is deserving of compassion and understanding. Sam McPherson had rejected his father in *Windy McPherson's Son* and George Willard followed

Sam's pattern of behavior in *Winesburg, Ohio*; in each case, however, Anderson's portrayal of the father was unsympathetic. But in "The Egg" Anderson presents a new image; although the narrator does not understand his father, he perceives that the man is worthy of love. For Anderson, the shadow of Irwin Anderson is coming into a clearer, more sympathetic focus. This shadowy figure will continue to elude Anderson and remain unknown.

This note of frustration at the hopelessness of the father's lot continues throughout *The Triumph of the Egg*. Each of the other protagonists is unable to penetrate his isolation even for moments, because there is no one like George Willard to whom he can turn, and the cumulative intensity of his frustrated bewilderment turns to despair. In "Unlighted Lamps," a young girl seeks love and understanding, first from her father and then from a young man. Repulsed and misunderstood, she is alone at the end, lost and unfulfilled. "Senility" portrays an old-young man who can cure "coughs, colds, consumption, and the sickness that bleeds," but not the sickness in his own heart. In "The Brown Coat" a college professor is able to understand the secrets of ancient civilizations, but not the secret that will enable love and understanding to grow between him and his wife. He is ". . . as alone as ever any man God made" in his despair.

Two of the stories, "Brothers" and "The Door of the Trap," show the fate of those who attempt to break down their barriers. In "Brothers," the old man who proclaims his kinship with others is called insane; in "The Door of the Trap," a college professor realizes that he is misunderstood, and, like Dr. Reefy in "Paper Pills," he withdraws to become a grotesque. The two sketches "War" and "Motherhood" reinforce and extend the despair that emanates from the lives of the old man and the professor.

A spinster's vain hope to find fulfillment in the new, fertile Midwest is portrayed in "The New Englander." The woman finds, instead, that she is imprisoned by the old, dead ideas and is condemned to infertility. Like the others she recognizes the futility of her efforts to find the understanding she needs.

In the last story, "Out of Nowhere into Nothing," Anderson epitomizes the hopelessness of his people. This is the story of a romantic young girl who, in her search for personal freedom and fulfillment, leaves her small town to go to the city. She gives up the search and returns to her home town convinced that the city is too dehumanized to satisfy her need for fulfillment. On returning to the town she hopes that somewhere in that more intimate environment there is understanding. But after thinking she has found it in the town, she realizes her folly and runs off into the night, into the emptiness that had characterized her life everywhere.

As Anderson concludes the volume with the statement that men can do nothing but run from life with "fleeing harried minds," he reiterates his present sense of futility and despair. In the earlier works he concluded with the faith that somehow his people might break through the barriers that had isolated them, but here he sees the future in terms as bleak as the past. At this point in Anderson's work, as in *Marching Men,* his characters are on the point of an irrational, futile rebellion against the forces that constrict them. Anderson determined to portray that rebellion in his next book, *Many Marriages.*

The Triumph of the Egg is, like *Winesburg, Ohio,* a solid achievement. Two of the stories, "I Want to Know Why" and "The Egg," are among Anderson's best; "Seeds," "The New Englander," and "Out of Nowhere into Nothing" are more complex but not executed as well. Anderson's style in the stories is uniform, and as close to reproduction of the Midwestern idioms and the rural American storytelling traditions as is possible, but at times structural awkwardness and hazy symbolism occur in the lesser stories. None of these stories is a failure, although the sustained reiteration of the theme makes the opening and closing prose poems redundant.

Anderson's constantly emphasized air of hopelessness detracts from the effectiveness of the volume. Before the final note of despair is struck, the reader's mind is almost calloused from its repetition. But the stories are about people—all different, all human, all effectively portrayed. These are, in effect, the people of Winesburg who have not found George Willard's ear, and because they have not, they are without hope. Therefore, just as the first story in the collection, "I Want to Know Why," voices a youthful, desperate plea for insight into the imponderability of human life, the last, "Out of Nowhere into Nothing," concludes with the hopeless confusion of the adult who has learned that she can never find that insight. An intensifying progression of accumulating despair links the two stories.

The overwhelming air of despair in the book coincided with Anderson's own mood. After the book had been published, he took the *Dial* prize money and went to New Orleans—alone. There he began work on a shorter version of *Many Marriages* for *Dial*. He wrote to Gertrude Stein that "I . . . have been writing like a man gone mad ever since I got off the train," and he began to see *Many Marriages* as a full-length novel. Late that spring, he returned to Chicago to make his final break with advertising and with Tennessee. After doing so he headed East in the summer.

His goal was New York, but his trip there was slow and uncertain; he was undergoing a soul-searching as intense as that which had brought him to nervous exhaustion in Elyria. Evidently recognizing the parallel with his earlier situation he stopped in Elyria ". . . to try to arrive at some sort of basis for self-criticism." He wandered; he saw that a new name replaced his on the paint factory sign; and unrecognized, he passed his old banker in the street. Even though this voyage to the past produced no answers, he now went on to New York.

In New York, he renewed acquaintanceship with the *Seven Arts* circle; he became close friends with Alfred Stieglitz; he saw a great deal of Paul Rosenfeld; and he met Elizabeth Prall, who was to become his third wife. The full-length manuscript of *Many Marriages* was finished that fall; the shorter version was appearing in *Dial*. He began to see Miss Prall frequently; soon they were in love. To the bookish young woman, he was a literary lion; to Anderson she was the anchor necessary to curb his restlessness and, at the same time, complement his increasing literary respectability. In February 1923, he went to Reno to divorce Tennessee.

Many Marriages was published at this time. In it Anderson resumes the offensive against the forces that have driven his people to despair. Resembling the assault of a decade ago, depicted in *Marching Men*, it is a headlong attack, doomed from its inception because it is instinctive rather than rational and blind rather than directed. In *Many Marriages*, Anderson focuses his bitterness on the "old thoughts and beliefs planted by dead men," the most serious of which is the perversion of the potentially good sex act into a secret sin.

The novel describes the attempt of John Webster, a small-town washing machine manufacturer, to break away from middle-class hypocrisy and find personal fulfillment. He leaves home, family, business, and social position to run off with his secretary after an overlong attempt, distorted by heavy-handed symbolism, to make his daughter understand. The novel is not, however, another retelling of Anderson's old rebellion against materialism, directed at sexual mores

rather than industrialism. Webster had inherited his beliefs as part
of his middle-class heritage, and there is no specific act that makes
him question them. Instead, he has an intuition, a vague sense that
something is wrong. Nor is Anderson using the book as a symbol of
the spirit of the intellectual revolt of the Chicago renaissance. Webster's grotesqueness, his long explanation, and his sense of futility at
the end make a great difference. His rebellion and its aftermath in
frustration have ramifications that the Chicago group failed to perceive. Anderson had by this time become aware of complexities unknown to him in Chicago.

Webster remains a grotesque to the end; spiritually he is related
to the people of *Winesburg, Ohio* and *The Triumph of the Egg,*
rather than to Sam McPherson and Beaut McGregor. He seeks
understanding from his daughter and his secretary, just as the people of Winesburg sought out George Willard, but neither woman
understands; and even though his secretary runs off with him, Webster remains isolated and baffled.

Webster's long explanation to his daughter of his behavior and
his frustration occupies much of the book; but it is not merely a
grotesque's plea for understanding or a plea for sexual liberation,
which critics have called it. Seen in its proper perspective, it is the
collective protest of the grotesques who have been distorted since
the dead ideas of dead men first started warping human personality.
The brutalization of sex by society is only one manifestation of the
many factors involved. Because Anderson couched this protest in
sexual terms, the symbol has been mistaken for the thing symbolized.
"How many marriages among people!" Anderson cries out as he regrets all the impotent relationships among men.

At the end of *Many Marriages,* Webster remains trapped, realizing that he still has not found understanding and that the secretary
at his side is a stranger; and, in all likelihood, things will be as they
were. Instead of walking confidently into the future, he ventures un-
certainly into the unknown. *Many Marriages,* like *The Triumph of
the Egg,* is a document of frustration and hopelessness. No longer
does Anderson believe that the individual can find fulfillment in rebellion. Rebellion is a beginning rather than an end, and once one
has begun to rebel, he has no choice except to go on searching.

The novel is not good; nor is it bad enough to consign it permanently to critical oblivion. The weaknesses are serious, especially in
the structural defect resulting from John Webster's long explanation

to his daughter. Actually, this incident *is* the novel, and the rest is mere framework. The incident itself has been so padded that it loses its value as a focal point and obscures the many merits of the book. Consequently, the novel suffers on two counts: artistically, from the distortion of its form, and ideologically, from its obscured theme.

It also suffers from the generally unsatisfactory use of symbols. The statue of the Virgin, the candles, and the "Jewel of Life," as used by Webster to symbolize innocence and hope, are redundant. The emphasis is placed on the appearance of the symbols rather than on their symbolic meaning, making them trite and useless; so much so, that Anderson himself abandons them after having given them prominence in Webster's long explanation. Webster's eccentricities, especially his nudity, serve a very limited purpose.

The novel was startling and controversial. Critical reception was good, as were early sales, and it was called a masterpiece by Theodore Dreiser and F. Scott Fitzgerald. But a strong reaction set in against its subject matter. It was banned in New England, libraries refused to buy it, and booksellers kept it under the counter. It was known as a dirty book, and puritan influences were strong enough to prevent its dissemination. Sales dwindled to nothing, and as a consequence, it has remained in oblivion. Yet, to ignore the book is unfortunate. Not only does it have a thematic statement that is simple but profound, but it occupies a critical position in the chronology of Anderson's work.

Anderson explained that an "irresistible impulse" compelled him to expand the *Dial* version into a novel, and it is perhaps for this reason that these defects occur so soon after the first-rate writing in *Winesburg, Ohio, Poor White,* and *The Triumph of the Egg.* More likely, however, the reason lies in factors growing out of Anderson's personal difficulties at the time. The book is an explosion, an ill-considered novel of rebellion arising out of his own frustration and despair.

Still another possible reason for the shortcomings in the book, indicated by his letters of the time, is that he was conscious of the fact that *Many Marriages,* like *Winesburg, Ohio,* might be considered a dirty book. In his desperate efforts to convey the idea that sexual frustration was a symbol of a more serious malady in man's life, he piled symbol on symbol in such confusion that his intended purpose was lost to his readers.

While *Many Marriages* ran its brief course, Anderson remained in Reno, establishing his residency in order to divorce Tennessee Mitchell. But Tennessee, who had maintained that marriage should be mutually liberating, refused to give her consent to a divorce, and Anderson remained in Nevada until January 1924, when she finally consented. Here he finished another collection of short stories, *Horses and Men,* and started the impressionistic memoir that was to become *A Story Teller's Story.* The mood of despair remained with him in spite of his enthusiasm for the desert and the mountains, and the enforced loneliness led him to start a re-examination of himself and his beliefs. At this time he wrote: "There is so little one man can do for another. What is to be said? What is to be done?" and again, "I know I do not want New York and the neurotics any more for a long, long time." Of himself he thought, "I've had too much prominence. It isn't any good. It's all bunk."

At the same time he wrote constantly to old friends, especially Gertrude Stein, Van Wyck Brooks, Alfred Stieglitz, and Jerome and Lucile Blum. He wrote primarily of himself but not about himself. As in John Webster's long explanation in *Many Marriages,* he was trying to articulate his beliefs in such a way that not only others could understand them but he himself as well. He wrote, "You see . . . I believe in this damn mixed-up country of ours. In an odd way I'm in love with it. And you get into it, in my sense of it, quite tremendously." His previous attempts to understand the American experience had led only to frustration and despair, and now, he was unwilling to admit the defeat that he feared.

Meanwhile, *Horses and Men* was published in the fall of 1923. The critical reception was generally enthusiastic, but Anderson paid little attention to it as he began to emerge slowly out of the hopelessness that was also expressed in this book. In this collection, as in *The Triumph of the Egg,* Anderson carries the sense of despair of the earlier volume so far that some of his people show touches of insanity as well as psychological torment. These stories, like those in *The Triumph of the Egg,* lose much of their significance when they are taken out of the context of the volume.

In *Horses and Men,* Anderson uses a foreword to set the thematic tone. His purpose, he makes clear, is the continued effort to probe beneath the dark surface of life and to get at its essence. He had begun such a search in *Winesburg, Ohio.* But almost immediately the self-doubts, uncertainties, and frustrations make themselves felt. "I had pushed myself off into a world where nothing has any existence," Anderson wrote. "It may be that my eyes are blind . . . . It may be I am deaf . . . . Now, alas, I am absorbed in looking at my own hands. With these nervous and uncertain hands may I really feel for the form of things concealed in the darkness?" His only hope for survival is to go on trying to discover what meaning there may be in life through the use of gentle, compassionate intuition.

As in *The Triumph of the Egg,* the foreword introduces a sense of frustrated bewilderment that descends into despair as the stories unfold. It is only in the last few tales that Anderson, almost unwillingly, displays a cautious and subdued optimism. For the most part, however, his people remain despairing until they seem ready for the same sort of mindless rebellion as waged by John Webster. However, they do not rebel; unlike Webster, they are too blinded by their despair to select any particular force and attack it. Another similarity to *The Triumph of the Egg* is the occasional appearance of a story that seems superficially humorous when lifted out of context, but here, too, Anderson has no interest in being funny; the predicament of his people is too serious for that.

This collection, like *The Triumph of the Egg,* opens with the story of a boy who likes horses and who finds that the world is infinitely more complex than the stables. In this story, "I'm a Fool," Anderson uses the theme of the adolescent's initiation as a signpost pointing to the ensuing adult narrator's recognition of the bewilderment that results from confusing appearance with reality. Here, as in "I Want to Know Why," the problem is too complex for the adolescent narrator. Anderson does not see it in any simpler terms either, although to him it is evident that such confusion apparently prohibits personal fulfillment forever.

The story is that of a boy growing into manhood as he follows the Ohio race track circuit. In the stables, working as a swipe, he lives a life that, while sometimes brutal and often crude, is nevertheless innocent, honest, and uncomplicated. On his day off he dresses up to go to the races as a spectator; stopping in a hotel bar, he sees a well-dressed young man, whom he resents, and to show his contempt for the dude, he pushes him aside and has two drinks of whiskey. At the track he meets a young lady and tells her lies about his background in order to impress her. Although she accepts him, he knows that because of the lies he has told her, he can never see her again. In the end, he comes to the conclusion that he had lied because of the whiskey, and he calls himself a fool; he calls the dude one, too, for causing him to lie. At this point, he is ready either to kick himself or to strike out at the dude, but he knows that it is futile to do either.

Here, as in all his race track stories, Anderson points out the dichotomy of appearance and reality. The boy resents the dude because he believes that the dude is striving to create an impression; yet, when the social situation demands it, the boy does the same, forgetting his belief that clothes do not make the man. His intuitive acceptance of reality had been distorted earlier when he had lied in the town saloons to impress the hangers-on, but the lying had been for fun and free drinks. In meeting the girl he instinctively lies again; this time, it is not for fun, but because he has entered a situation in which society declares that appearances are important. Suddenly realizing that he has been forced into ignoring reality, he is ready for an irrational assault, but he has no idea what to attack. Although earlier, the appearance of social stratification had disgusted him both at home and in the bar, he accepts the girl and her companions at face value and attempts to know them on what appears to be their level, thus accepting society's emphasis on appearance in place of his own standards of intrinsic worth. In drinking and lying, both of which were acceptable in his own world of the race track, he has violated the social standards that he had temporarily accepted, and he recognizes that because he has violated them, his punishment must be the rejection that society imposes in such cases. But he still does not feel that the acts of drinking and lying are wrong in themselves. His paradoxical resentment and his confusion result from the complexity of conflicting values that he is unable to resolve.

Behind the boy's predicament the adult narrator is evident and almost omnipresent, as in "I Want to Know Why." This was in the days, we are told by the narrator, "before prohibition and all that foolishness," so the narrator is actually an adult, yet his bewilderment had continued from adolescence to manhood. He recognizes that there is a difference between the appearance and reality of intrinsic worth, just as he had when he was a youth; but the problem is not only unresolved as yet; it is apparently unresolvable. The cause of his failure to find fulfillment and love still eludes him; he can only resent the dude, as the symbol of society, and his own temporary foolishness.

Although this is one of Anderson's most widely anthologized stories, it is not as carefully constructed as "I Want to Know Why," which, essentially, treats the same theme. The adult narrator is less obviously seen, and for this reason, if the narrator as narrator is actually an adult, continued adult bewilderment is almost lost in the boy's adolescent complaint. Also, Anderson's style, usually at its best in the race track narratives, is more forced, more deliberately and consciously adolescent, than in "I Want to Know Why." In his efforts to adopt the mask of a lovesick youth he has lessened the thematic impact of despair that the volume professes. However, these stylistic and structural shortcomings contribute to the character of the boy, making him pathetic and appealing; but they also contribute to a misplaced emphasis in interpretation that sees the humor inherent in puppy love but does not see the adult bewilderment behind it.

In the following story, "The Triumph of a Modern," Anderson examines the same confusion of values in terms of the modernist revolt of the Chicago liberation. In this story, a "liberated" young man who prides himself on his rejection of puritanical standards of behavior, writes an intimate letter to a maiden aunt whom he has never seen. Deliberately employing the word *breasts,* rather than the more conventional *bosom* in a carefully contrived emotional passage designed to convey a love for her that he does not feel, he so appeals to her frustrated maternal and sexual instincts that she wills him her fortune.

In this story, Anderson points out that even rebellion against the dead ideas of the past may be so false and deliberately dishonest that it may be used as a tool for crude and selfish purposes, thus obviating an honest attack on the forces that imprison man. Anderson's new objections to the philosophy of the liberation movement are more than mere restlessness, as this story indicates; he is convinced that the movement had become an end in itself, rather than a means to the end of eventual human fulfillment. The moderns have had their victory, the title implies, but they have given up the war.

It would be interesting to know if Anderson had in mind the reception of *Winesburg, Ohio* and *Many Marriages* when he wrote this story. Among liberated circles, both works were seen as calls for rebellion against puritanical sex standards. It is evident from Anderson's disappointment at those narrow interpretations that he had a far greater and more inclusive problem in mind. Such critical reaction must have given him a great deal of insight into the failure of the movement which, as he indicated in letters from Reno, had attracted neurotics rather than seekers. In "The Triumph of a Modern," he condemns the movement for the same inability to distinguish between appearance and reality, means and ends, as the moderns had condemned conventional society.

"I'm a Fool" and "The Triumph of a Modern" set the structural and thematic patterns that unify the collection. In the remainder of the stories, Anderson alternates, as he has in these two, between a rural, agricultural setting and an urban, commercial setting; and with the exception of the last story, each one is designed to be mutually complementary. He shows that human fulfillment is defeated by shortcomings in man and society, common to both country and city environments.

In the first pair of stories each young man is defeated because he cannot or does not distinguish between appearance and reality, but instead, distorts reality in order to gain in appearance, not recognizing that the resulting confusion of values will cut him off from fulfillment forever. The boy in "I'm a Fool" tries to gain social approval, and the young modern in "The Triumph of a Modern" gains an inheritance, but in so doing, they have both rejected truth and erected the barriers that imprison them.

"Unused" and "A Chicago Hamlet" continue this pairing of setting and theme; both of them are concerned with people whose efforts to carry through an honest rebellion result in tragedy. The first, set in Bidwell, Ohio, is the story of a young girl from a disreputable family whose efforts to rise above it are frustrated by misinterpretation. In despair she runs into the lake and drowns. The narrator is filled with compassion as he views the drowned girl's body after its recovery, and the memory of her bedraggled ostrich feather remains with him as a symbol of her frustrated attempt to find beauty. It is a memory that throws him into continued despair. The second story, "A Chicago Hamlet," tells the story of a man who had failed in his rebellion and ". . . had gone the same road I and all the men about me were no doubt going, the road of surrender to ugliness and to dreary meaningless living." His efforts to break out of his path of surrender are frustrated to the point where, dead spiritually, he can only drink and say, "It is horrible stuff, this whiskey, eh, but after all this is a horrible town." Out of the despair engendered by this tragedy, the narrator can only cry out:

Millions of us live on the vast Chicago West Side, where all streets are equally ugly and where the streets go on and on forever, out of nowhere into nothing. We are tired, tired! What is it all about?

The narrator of "A Chicago Hamlet" re-emphasizes the despair of the narrator of "Unused," as he recounts his friend's drunken attempt to escape his recurrent dream of a slender and beautiful woman who, as she comes closer, is revealed to be broken in pieces, a grim caricature of beauty. In both stories the rebellion of the grotesques results only in personal tragedy.

In each of the next pair of stories, "The Man Who Became a Woman" and "Milk Bottles," Anderson writes of a young man who has been forced to deny his individuality. Here the penalties of nonconformity are exacted in moments of horror; in the first instance, among the discarded bones in an abandoned slaughterhouse, and in the latter, the grimness of rubbish heaps in the shadow of a tenement.

"The Man Who Became a Woman" is one of Anderson's best stories, ranking with "The Egg" and "I Want to Know Why." Another story dealing with an adolescent lover of race horses and race track naturalness, this goes beyond both the adolescent's initiation and the concept of homosexuality implied in the title. In it, Anderson comes close to identifying the source of much of man's difficulty as the two sides of his nature, the brutality of masculinity and the compassion of femininity, clash within him.

This story, like "Unused," is told by an adult narrator looking back on an incident that took place in his youth. He has never understood the significance of the incident, yet he is driven to describe it in detail. The story ends with the narrator still plagued by the feeling that in accepting the dictates of convention he has surrendered a major part of his personality and has cut himself off from fulfillment. The nullifying factor to his surrender is hidden somewhere in the incident itself, as he well realizes, but even now, in adulthood, he is unable to find it.

The story recounts the experience of a night on the race track circuit. The boy, left alone at the track, decides to go to town. Stopping in a rough bar, he remembers past dreams in which he thought he was a girl. Looking into the mirror behind the bar he sees that his face looks like a girl's, and afraid, he decides to leave. A giant brute of a man enters and starts a fight; the ensuing disorder gives the boy an opportunity to flee. Still frightened, he runs

back to the stables to sleep; but he is awakened by two drunken
swipes who mistake him for a girl. Again frightened, he runs off into
the darkness, and falling into a pile of bones behind an old slaughterhouse, he remains hidden for the night. His terror is so strong that
"It burned all that silly nonsense about being a girl right out of me";
the next day he leaves the race track forever.

Anderson has kept this complex symbolic structure under careful
control. The comparison between horses and men is used as a contrast
between simple beauty and distorted ugliness, as in the earlier race
track stories, and it provides the opportunity for expression of
Anderson's bitterness: "A race horse isn't like a human being. He
won't stand for it to have to do his work in any rotten ugly kind of
a dump the way a man will, and he won't stand for the smells a man
will either." Such a view of the nature of man is bitter enough, but
Anderson goes beyond it.

Man's lot is hopeless, he points out, because he permits and even
encourages the brutal side of his nature to destroy and overwhelm
his feeling of understanding, compassion, and intuition. As the boy's
reaction in the saloon indicates, society trains us to interpret these
traits as degeneracy, and in order to live within society's framework
one is forced not only to deny them but to destroy them in himself.
In this story Anderson is not writing only of the tortured who revolt
against society, as in the preceding pair of stories, but also of the
majority of men who have been forced to deny part of their natures
and to live as grotesque caricatures of themselves.

Such an attempt might have been offensive, as *Many Marriages*
was to so many people, because "The Man Who Became a Woman"
has strong overtones of one of society's strongest taboos. This has
been considered a story of latent homosexuality rather than the
duality of man's nature, but Anderson's careful execution makes
such an interpretation impossible to the perceptive reader. He points
out through his narrator that appearances are not indicative of the
nature of underlying reality: ". . . a man here don't dare own up
he loves another man, I've found out, and they are afraid to admit
such feelings to themselves even. I guess they're afraid it may be
taken to mean something it don't need to at all."

This statement implies, too, that Anderson is permitting the re-
emergence of a semblance of hope in the thematic structure of the
volume, in spite of the almost overwhelming evidence he has compiled
to point out its futility. Here, the narrator catches a glimpse of the

necessary distinctions between appearance and reality mainly because he has intuitively recognized beauty. The fact that he is compelled to tell the story in adulthood indicates that he knows that somewhere in the incident he can re-discover truth. But as the story ends, the narrator still fails to find its ultimate meaning and remains spiritually deformed as a result.

Paired with this story is "Milk Bottles," a reiteration of the same theme. A young advertising writer tries to write what he feels is true, but the lies by which he earns his living and the grimness of his surroundings make it impossible for him to recognize either truth or beauty. Eventually, the lies of the boosters become truth for him. The lament of lost humanity bemoaning its hopelessness, implicit in the background of the story, makes the young man's tragedy only a part of a much greater tragedy: an actress, skilled in make-believe, comments that " 'we live such damned lives, we do, and we work in such a town! A dog is better off!'," and behind the advertising slogan that proclaims milk as " 'The health and freshness of a whole countryside. . . .' " the milk is sour in the bottles standing on window sills. Here Anderson portrays a humanity made up of individuals who are tortured and lost, unable to rescue themselves because there is no means by which they can escape.

The last pair of stories returns to the theme of the futility in attempting to rebel or escape. In the first story, "The Sad Horn Blowers," a young man flees the dehumanizing influences of a small town only to find himself condemned in the city to a lifetime of drilling meaningless holes in meaningless pieces of metal. All he can do is pick up his trumpet and join others in a muted and futile gesture of protest. In the second, "The Man's Story," a married man runs off with another woman, and they take refuge in the anonymity of a large city. She is murdered, and he is arrested, but later acquitted through another's confession. Nevertheless he might better have been hanged: "The man had come up out of the sea of doubt, had grasped for a time the hand of the woman, and with her hand in his had floated for a time upon the surface of life—but now he felt himself again sinking down into the sea." He had glimpsed fulfillment, but it eluded him. Perhaps this is the end of John Webster's rebellion, as Anderson suggests in the conclusion of *Many Marriages*.

"The Sad Horn Blowers" is interesting for the light that it sheds on Anderson's changing view of the father-son relationship. From the son's complete misunderstanding of his father in *Windy McPher-son's Son,* the presentation had changed, in "The Egg," to the son's recognition of the father as a grotesque deserving of compassion. In "The Sad Horn Blowers," Anderson moves beyond mere compassion and portrays the son learning to understand his father through in-tuition and finally coming to identify his life with his father's. This is only possible after the son has experienced the same sort of frus-tration as the father. This new point of view suggests that Anderson realized, at this point, that he, like his father, can find no satisfaction except in his stories. In the last story, "An Ohio Pagan," Anderson returns to the rural scene in an account ending on a note of optimism. Unpaired with a similar story using a city theme, "An Ohio Pagan" culminates the gradual re-emergence of faith that had begun in "The Man Who Became a Woman." After exposure to dehumanizing in-fluences of both city and village, the young protagonist of "An Ohio Pagan" decides that he can find fulfillment through love and under-standing, but he must first learn to identify them. This belief is not in the easy-answer manner of the earlier novels, however, because Anderson is no longer certain that such a search will actually result in finding meaning. He implies that man may find satisfaction in the search even though it never ends. Here he returns in spirit to the ending of *Marching Men:* perhaps the purpose of man's life lies not in the attainment of any eventual victory but in the spirit with which he goes down to defeat.

In *Horses and Men,* Anderson has maintained a high level of literary achievement. The stories are written in the *Winesburg* man-ner, emphasizing revelation of character through moments of intense experience and depending for their effect upon this revelation rather than upon any significant plot structure. He has also continued the stylistic technique of the earthy Midwestern storyteller, with the same generally good effects. As a result, two of the stories, "I'm a Fool" and "The Man Who Became a Woman," are among his best, and others, including "A Chicago Hamlet" and "The Sad Horn Blowers," are very good. None is a complete failure, although some, like "Unused," would have profited from a clearer focus on motiva-tion and the meaning of symbols. As the shifts between city and country indicate, Anderson's grotesques do not result from values peculiar to either locale, but to society as a whole.

With this volume, Anderson concludes the search that he had started in *Winesburg, Ohio:* the attempt to determine the ultimate relationship between man and his time by examining the effects of society on the people he has known. In his attempt to know these effects through his intuitive perception of the essence of each individual, Anderson has found that the individual is helpless as a result of what society has done to him; he has come to realize the complexity of the social structure that has isolated and deformed man's spirit; and he has been forced to admit the futility of open rebellion against those social standards. Despair, however, cannot be maintained indefinitely, and, although at the end of *Horses and Men,* Anderson still sees no hope for the ultimate liberation of the individual, he has begun to regain his faith that somehow man can come to know and understand himself and his fellows, and that through such understanding will come a worthwhile and satisfying existence.

With his divorce won from Tennessee and *Horses and Men* well received, Anderson left Reno early in 1924 with much of his despair behind him. He married Elizabeth Prall in the hope that he would find a mutually fulfilling relationship, and with his new wife he began a period of wandering across the American countryside, hoping that he might yet find a place and a people who rejected the values of materialism.

In his work and his personal life he again started in a new direction; his new rebellion against the easy path of "liberation" was completed. He carried with him in his wanderings a partially completed autobiographical manuscript. Behind his cheerfulness, however, there was a note of anxiety. "Don't ask too much," he wrote. "The staleness exists, the flatness. Often enough it gets into a man and infects him like a disease. It is a disease, I think, crawling fear of what? Life, I fancy." Nevertheless, hope had returned, and he also wrote that "I feel like a man recovering from a long illness, every day more ready for work now."

5

INTROSPECTION AND
IDENTIFICATION

D URING the mid-twenties Anderson's published works were almost entirely autobiographical or semiautobiographical, including *Dark Laughter,* his major novel of the period. Two of these works, *A Story Teller's Story* and *Tar: A Midwest Childhood,* are attempts to evaluate and interpret his own experience against the backdrop of the Midwest between the end of the Civil War and the early 1920s; *Sherwood Anderson's Notebook* examines his experiences as writer in America; and *Dark Laughter* is the fictionalized account of his rebellion against the modern liberation movement.

The years between 1923 and 1927 were a time of uncertainty, searching, and wandering for Anderson although his marriage to Elizabeth Prall promised to be successful and he was writing almost constantly, finishing one manuscript and turning immediately to the next. He and Elizabeth lived in Berkeley, California, for a few months before going on to New Orleans, where they intended to live permanently. Finances were tight, as usual; *Horses and Men* was not selling; and Anderson began to feel the pressures that would again take him from his writing, but he was resolved to do anything rather than go back to advertising.

Meanwhile he was determined to continue in his attempt to understand the meaning of the American experience as he had known it. He had to rid himself of recurring uncertainties about his life; especially about the writing career that had almost forced itself upon him, about the value of his work, and about his presumption that he could do his material justice. Shortly after his return to New Orleans he finished *A Story Teller's Story,* but he was very uncertain about it; he wrote to his brother Karl:

Don't know about *A Story Teller's Story*, whether I got what I was after or not. I didn't try to set down obvious facts, only tried to get the spirit of something.

The spirit of that something he was trying to get was insight into the meaning of his own life as it had been shaped by experience. To find this insight he chose the technique of intuitively examining the underlying meaning of the appearance of people and events. In such a technique, factual credence is unimportant, except as the roughest sort of guide, and in practice it must be ignored in order to penetrate beyond it to the essence of things. The resulting work cannot be considered a factual account of Anderson's life, but it does reveal the essence of individuality, and the relationships between man and man, man and circumstances, and man and ideas. This approach had worked for Anderson in fiction and he had no reason to suppose that it would not work in dealing with the meaning of his own life.

In this instance, Anderson was not attempting to write either fiction or autobiography; he points out in the book, "I have perhaps lied now and then . . . but have not lied about the essence . . ." because, he explains, "In the world of fancy . . . no man is ugly. Man is ugly in fact only." As a result, *A Story Teller's Story* uses fact only as a point of departure from whence intuitive perception takes over. The result does not fit conveniently into either of the conventional categories of fact or fiction, and critics who have attempted to categorize it have missed Anderson's purpose.

In it Anderson is attempting to solve one problem: that of his own identity. Thus far, his life had been a series of rejections on every level, ranging from his initial rejection of the small town to his rejection of the city, from his rejection of business ethics to rejection of the ethics of the liberation, and from rejection of his father to rejection of the women he had married. At 48, he had found no stability, because each of his experiences had proven to be disappointing and frustrating. Now he was starting to look back, to re-examine those experiences in the light of what had come after, and to try to determine whether or not his rejections were sound; if they were not, he wanted to find out what he had missed that had made him what he was. Then, perhaps, he could find out whether he was a mere idler and player with words, as his recurring fears told him, or whether he was really on the path that would lead to his understanding of the human experience, if he persevered.

That Anderson was re-interpreting the facts of his earlier life is readily apparent in *A Story Teller's Story*. The miserable childhood that he had portrayed in all of his novels except *Many Marriages* is gone, and in its place is a life that was hard but not heartless; poor but not poverty-stricken. Appearance, he decides almost at once, had been deceiving him for a long time, and he had been failing to see the warmth of intimate family relations that compensated for the absence of material things. The father brought romance into the life of the family; the mother brought love and comfort; the brothers and the sister provided strength and confidence; and the legendary grandmother brought the security of earthy origins. In such a portrayal, the contrast with that family presented in *Windy McPherson's Son* is obvious. The facts are substantially the same, but behind them, Anderson has begun to see a close and meaningful human relationship that he had unwittingly ignored.

The most striking change in this portrayal from that of the early years is the one wrought in the character of his father, Irwin Anderson. As seen through the eyes of Sam McPherson, the father was a failure, a windbag, and a symbol of personal inadequacy, but this characterization was a ludicrous, rather than a vicious one. Anderson's reversal of this interpretation is not sudden, but it is a view that he had been fumbling for, perhaps unconsciously, since he found himself following Irwin's footsteps in rejecting the practical life for the impractical and the world of facts for the world of dreams. This new portrayal gives Anderson a sense of identity and purpose; he draws Irwin Anderson as a technologically displaced person of the 1890s, just as he had begun to regard himself as the counterpart of such a person in the 1920s. Thus, Irwin Anderson is presented as the archetype of the artist in America:

> My father lived in a land and in a time when what one later begins to understand a little as the artist in man could not by any possibility be understood by his fellows. Dreams then were to be expressed in building railroads and factories, in boring gas wells, stringing telegraph poles. There was room for no other dream and since father could not do any of these things he was an outlaw in his community. The community tolerated him. His own sons tolerated him.

In actuality, Irwin was not regarded as an outlaw in Clyde; in spite of his improvidence and his well-known bouts with the bottle, he was liked and occasionally was even a leader. However, it is an image that

Anderson could accept because he sensed himself to be a double out-law, both for his rejection of materialism and for the misinterpreta-tion by critics and public of *Winesburg, Ohio* and *Many Marriages*. It was at this point that he had asked himself, "Had I a sex ob-session? Was I a goner?" and in recognizing the misunderstanding that Irwin met because he rejected the standards of his time, he saw himself also as a victim of his contemporaries. He had been true to himself and to his view of life; and was misunderstood as a result.

Identification of himself with his father goes beyond this sort of rationalization, however, to place Anderson in the time-out-of-mind folklore tradition of the storyteller—the man who belongs to no group or society because his calling transcends both as it deals with the essence of life. This is the rationale that Anderson needed at this time in order to continue the writing that had become the center and the purpose of his existence.

As a result of this changed view of his father, Anderson had with-drawn his earliest rejection, that of his father, and in *A Story Teller's Story* he subsequently examines other rejections and values that he had previously accepted unquestioningly. In rambling, formless style, as the impressions occur to him, he recounts the impact of pride of workmanship, of the new philosophy of success, of cheap, impressive construction upon himself and his times. In each of the recreated in-cidents Anderson questions himself: had he recognized what each actually meant, or had he accepted the appearance of things as in-dicative of their intrinsic worth? He is not certain as he writes, so he passes on to his other acceptances and rejections.

His youthful adventures along the race track circuit, his early laboring years in Chicago, and his Spanish-American War experi-ences are treated in detail. In his youth, he deduces, the real desire for material success was implanted in him through a Judge Turner, who was for him the same sort of father image that John Telfer was for Sam McPherson; and as a result he made his first rejection —of simple and natural values—as he went to Chicago to follow the glitter of the things that a materialistic society promised. During the early Chicago years he was confused; on one hand he saw hard-ness, brutality, and poverty; on the other he was still blinded by the dream of conventional success. He re-interpreted the myth he had previously accepted from Judge Turner as he saw values he had carried from Clyde destroyed around him: the strong mother love of the town was replaced by gin in the city; the respected merchant, a kindly man in the town, became a single-minded exploiter in the city. The only values that had any permanency, he found at this point, were those of human relationships, and these were threatened by his life in the factory. His ensuing dilemma was temporarily solved by the Spanish-American War.

The army experience, as he looks back, was also misleading; he had mistaken unity among the men for comradeship. He had tried in *Marching Men,* to make reality out of a dream, he concludes, as he asks himself, "Is all feeling of comradeship, of brotherhood between many men, a little absurd?" He had, he realizes now, confused the appearance of unity with its reality, just as he had confused so many other things.

His rejection of commercial success and his decision to become a writer are examined in *A Story Teller's Story,* including his dramatic exit from the paint factory as it has been incorporated into the Anderson myth. Discrepancies with the actual circumstances abound here also, but they are immaterial; Anderson is trying to determine the motives that brought about that rejection, too, and he is trying to find the meaning of his literary career. He decides that his motive for rejecting industrialism and for writing stem from the same source; industrialism is dehumanizing, but he is driven by the desire to humanize. In his writing he is attempting two things: restoring crafts-manship in literature and at the same time probing beneath the stand-ardized surface of human life in order to find its real meaning.

The last major rejection that he reviews is his determination to ignore the personally and artistically destructive forces of both the liberation movement and the literary market place. At this point his discouragement, his frustrations, and his persistent doubts about his abilities are most in evidence, but he recognizes himself as his father's son and knows that he can do nothing else but write. Here he records his decision to look to the South in the almost optimistic hope that he can find a place there to do his work honestly. As he makes the decision, uncertainty remains, but the book ends on a note of faith. The "spirit of something" that he was trying to get was the spirit he needed to carry himself through the doubt and despair that plagued him in both his writing and his personal life.

In *A Story Teller's Story,* Anderson has fused both his personal life and his writing career into a mutually justifying and mutually supporting whole. Through his identification of himself with the re-interpreted image of his father he has rationalized away his fear that he is a "goner," a degenerate, because he rejects conventionally acceptable standards of behavior and literary subject matter. In constructing his new image, he has made Irwin a storyteller, rather than a drunkard and a braggart, who like himself, found meaning in the life of the imagination. He has justified the instability of his own personal and family life because he, like Irwin, follows a calling beyond society's dictates, and he has emerged with a new sense of mission for himself in his role of storyteller.

From his point of view *A Story Teller's Story* was a success because it did allow him to find a sense of personal identity by leading him ". . . toward understanding of whatever may be beautiful and fine in life, my own life and other lives," but he did not expect the book to sell because it was such a personal thing. In this he was right, but, as in the past, he did not anticipate the criticism that would be leveled at it for its looseness of structure and factual treatment.

The form of the book is a direct result of the intuitive approach that Anderson has employed. This approach is dependent on bursts of illumination or of insight into the true meaning of appearance, for its effectiveness. On the other hand, it is not capable of effectively sustaining a prolonged narrative of any kind. The short works used this approach to great advantage, but in *A Story Teller's Story*, it results in a loose, unconnected narrative that is uneven in execution. Individual passages, especially those on the machine age, on the return to Elyria, and on the thoughts of America inspired by the cathedral at Chartres, are among his best work, but the unsatisfactory passages detract from its over-all effectiveness.

Structurally and stylistically, *A Story Teller's Story* is an approach to the oral storytelling tradition as Anderson learned it from his father, and this, too, accounts for the looseness of structure. Rambling, digressive, and disorganized on the surface, it pauses to explore a side issue or to explain a bit of seemingly irrelevant background. Then suddenly these seeming irrelevancies become pertinent, the narrative has moved forward, and a point has been made. While this technique is sometimes exasperating, it is in keeping with the tradition with which Anderson identified himself. He had rejected slickness and superficiality, and his rejection is supported by his return to this old and authentic tradition.

A Story Teller's Story solved, at least temporarily, Anderson's doubts about the worth of what he was doing and the honesty of his decisions, but it did not solve his need for money—he did have a family to support. But he was determined not to go back to advertising, so he compromised by beginning immediately on *Dark Laughter,* meanwhile making arrangements to go on a lecture tour during the winter of 1925. However, in spite of his financial difficulties, he seemed happy after having purged himself of his artistic doubts and fears. To Paul Rosenfeld he wrote:

> The new book flows like a real river, so far . . . I'm at it hard anyway, and the days have joy in them. I've an idea there are fields ahead in which I haven't tried walking before.

After finishing *Dark Laughter* he became depressed again: "I'm utterly gloomy myself, always am when I have published a book. . . . Also I am gloomy about the new novel. It is on a shelf in my workshop." What was really bothering him, however, was his reputation among the general public as a salacious writer and his fear of facing these same people from the lecture platform:

> I am known as a dangerous man . . . . I think *Many Marriages* did it. The whole mood is one out of which I have quite passed now, but the public does not know that. It seems to them that when they come toward me I do something terrible. . . . They fear I will piss against the leg of the man who is introducing me or bring on the stage a lady and do her violence there to promote the higher life. . . . I can't make out whether they want me to do some such violence or are really afraid I will.

Even more than these problems, however, he was again beset by the old question that had bothered him before he had finished *A Story Teller's Story*: after his rejections, what then? At loose ends while waiting for the tour to begin, he fretted about it: "What is really puzzling is that I feel that the publication of *A Story Teller's Story* marked a period for me. I have been so much a naked man walking through the streets after all. Now I begin to want clothes again." Already he was prepared to return to the probing of his past in *Tar: A Midwest Childhood,* for which he had begun to make notes.

Meanwhile, he went on tour during January and February, 1925, and as much as he enjoyed traveling about again, seeing new places and meeting new people, he was depressed; he felt that lecturing was somehow dishonest, and he was eager to be at the new book.

Nevertheless, the tour was successful, and in *The Modern Writer,* which contains the text of the principal lecture he delivered at each place, he attempts to define the rationale behind his writing career. The writer, he points out, is caught in the same dilemma that all of America has been in for years: the necessity of choosing between commercial success and honest craftsmanship. The former, he says, is sought by writers who are dishonest, while the latter is executed by ". . . workmen whose materials are human lives. . . ." The true modern writer is one who is attempting to ". . . get back into his own hands some control over the tools of and materials of his craft." If he is honest, all the writer can want or expect is the freedom to do his work, and he should not ask for more. "The real reward I fancy lies just in the work itself, nowhere else. If you cannot get it there, you will not get it at all . . . . You are undertaking a task that can never be finished. The longest life will be too short to ever really get you anywhere near what you want."

In March the lecturing ordeal was over, and from his home in New Orleans, he could write "Am working again, the pen flying. I lectured, I saw people . . . . Made a little money and often an ass of myself." Preparing *Dark Laughter* for publication and working on *Tar: A Midwest Childhood,* absorbed his time and energies; he had signed a five-year contract with Horace Liveright that would take care of his immediate financial worries, and in restless moments he and Elizabeth took short trips through the South.

In the fall of 1925, while he was finishing *Tar,* *Dark Laughter* was published. In it Anderson had tried to convey "The neuroticism, the hurry and self-consciousness of modern life, and back of it the easy, strange laughter of the blacks." The novel is the story of the latest of his rejections which in effect, was the rejection of rejection. Anderson reiterates his disenchantment with the shallowness and meaninglessness of the supposedly emancipated circles of Chicago and New York, including the kind of marriage such a movement produces. He again rejects middle-class values; and he begins to return in spirit to the unspoiled primitive life that he had accepted in *A Story Teller's Story* and was redefining in *Tar.*

Anderson sets the tone for *Dark Laughter* in a preliminary sketch written in the *Winesburg* manner. Here, in the portrait of a minor character, Sponge Martin—a primitive craftsman who refuses to surrender to the new age, either his sense of a job well done or his individuality—he shows how life might be lived in simple, uncom-

plicated, and honest directness. Martin appears and reappears in the
novel as the symbol of the uncorrupted wise man: apparently an
outcast, but in reality a free man, as are the Negroes who form the
novel's background. The protagonist is Bruce Dudly. He had been
John Stockton of Chicago, but in changing his identity he had
rejected conventional standards, as had John Webster, and had gone
beyond that rebellion to reject rebellion as an end in itself. The
novel traces his attempts to find fulfillment and liberation after the
last of these rebellions.

In Chicago as Stockton, Dudly had been an advertising man, a
member of the liberation group, and a partner in a childless modern
marriage that, like Anderson's own marriage to Tennessee Mitchell,
was nothing more than a convenient legal arrangement. But advertising offended his growing sense of craftsmanship and the integrity
of words; the liberation group was so busy being free that it had
no time to go beyond freedom; and the marriage had given him
no fulfillment. Anderson points out the sterility of the latter two in
a sharp illustration: Dudly's wife is a writer; a vivid scene on a
street corner strikes her as significant, and she starts to make it into
a story, but she is unable to finish writing it. Although she has
caught the surface of the scene, she is incapable of capturing its
essence because she cannot understand it, and the story remains a
meaningless fragment. The bitter undercurrent is as strong here as
it is in the short stories Anderson wrote during his last Chicago
years; he punctuates his indictment with an acid comment, "For
the sake of art, eh?"

Anderson, in a series of skillfully handled flashbacks, gives a
surface portrayal of the Chicago liberation movement which makes
it appear to be an honest attempt to find a meaningful life through
a movement devoted to free self-expression. This surface picture is
largely responsible for the novel's initial reception as an affirmation
of the modernist movement; it also accounts for the more recent
interpretations that see Anderson as naive in his regard for the
movement. But both the earlier and more recent critics ignore Anderson's treatment in the flashbacks. His portrayal is deliberately
superficial, it makes no attempt to penetrate beneath the surface to
lay bare the essence as he does in his customary intuitive approach.
By using this technique, Dudly's wife becomes the vehicle through
which the impotence of the movement's people and the shallowness
of the movement are revealed. The rest of the novel is concerned

with Dudly's search for fulfillment. Leaving his marriage, the move-ment, and his job, he heads down the Illinois River toward the Mississippi, New Orleans, and a renewed sense of identification with America, convinced, ". . . that he, in common with almost all American men, had got out of touch with things—stones lying in fields, the fields themselves, houses, trees, rivers, factory walls, tools, women's bodies. . . ." In New Orleans he is fascinated by the foreign air and by the Negroes, but he is unable to know them. He returns anonymously to the Midwestern town where he was born, gets a job in the same factory as Sponge Martin, has an affair with the factory owner's wife. When she becomes pregnant, he runs off with her, presumably escaping to fulfillment. But in the background her Negro servants laugh mockingly and wisely as they recognize the futility of the attempted elopement.

Like all of Anderson's earlier novels, *Dark Laughter* is a story of conscious and deliberate rebellion and rejection; in this case, Dudly's rebellion against the superficialities of liberation and the manufac-turer's wife's rejection of her sterile and shallow marriage. Like all the novels, except *Many Marriages*, the conclusion seems opti-mistic as the couple choose fulfillment over sterility. But Anderson uses the mocking laughter of the Negroes to point out that the elope-ment is a gesture of rebellion rather than the achievement of free-dom. The novel has no real ending, and the impression remains, as at the end of *Poor White* and *Many Marriages*, that there is a much longer and more significant story to follow. In spite of the couple's acceptance of each other as human beings, and in spite of Dudly's confidence that somehow he would find meaningful work, the laugh of the Negro servants is as mocking as the factory whistles that accompanied Hugh McVey's decision in *Poor White*. But in spite of the doubts, Anderson feels that rejection is the only means whereby one can hope to find his way to eventual understanding and fulfill-ment; integrity demands that one follow that road, regardless of whether it leads to success or not. At this point Anderson could see no other meaning in man's life.

Structurally, the novel is very much like its predecessors, espe-cially *Many Marriages* and *Poor White*, in that Anderson devotes a substantial portion of the middle section to a long background digression that is actually irrelevant. In his efforts to incorporate as much of the atmosphere of the times into the novel, he gives a description, through flashback, of the shallowness and decadence of post-World War I international society. This description, however, becomes more than a contrast to the forceful, primitive, and meaningful life; it becomes a distraction from the main purpose of the novel. From a structural viewpoint, the attempt at the flashback technique fails in this connection. It does not broaden the base of his objections to the superficiality of society, because it is too remote from the Midwestern sterility that he is castigating. As a result it leads the reader into irrelevant and misleading byways that de-emphasize his intention to focus upon the breakdown of the liberation movement.

Stylistically the novel is a departure from the solid prose of *Poor White* and the collections of shorter works; it follows the disjointed technique of *Many Marriages* to the point where it loses the spontaneity of Anderson's Midwestern idiom and syntax and seems contrived. Occasionally, however, the Midwesterner takes command over the unhappy stylistic innovations, as in the Sponge Martin sketch, and the writing is as good as any in *Winesburg*. One wishes he had continued in that vein.

Anderson acknowledged that while writing *Dark Laughter,* he was influenced by James Joyce: "I think as a matter of prose experiment you will sense what Mr. Joyce was driving at when you read *Dark Laughter.* . . . I very frankly took his experiment as a starting place for the prose rhythm of the book." What Anderson did not realize was that his own earlier experimentation had led him to a style that had become his own, and that the Joycean imitation was actually hindering rather than advancing his career as a prose craftsman. The result is unsatisfactory imitation rather than solid originality.

It is unfortunate that Ernest Hemingway chose to parody this novel in *The Torrents of Spring*. Although the result was humorous, it was inept writing, and it indicates that Hemingway, like other writers of the period, had accepted the Anderson stereotype as the celebrator of the liberation. Other misinterpretations have resulted from viewing the novel in the light of that stereotype. Oscar Cargill, for example, sees Anderson's characters in *Dark Laughter* as intellectuals and the novel as essentially a story of contrast between the loves of the intellectuals Dudly and Aline and those of the unintellectual Negroes.[1] However, it is evident that both Dudly and

---

[1] Oscar Cargill, *Intellectual America* (New York, 1941), p. 329.

Aline have rejected the neurotic excesses and limitations of the Chicago liberation, the only intellectual life they know, and they are trying to find a new freedom uncomplicated by the jargon and the superficialities that Cargill points out. Mistakes such as these are easy to make because of the stylistic lapses and structural defects of the novel, but they are unnecessary.

The most serious criticism that can be leveled against Anderson in this novel is thoughtlessness. It is the basic trouble with *Many Marriages,* and its reoccurrence here results in formlessness and in the inability to carry rebellion through to whatever follows it. That something does follow is clearly implied, but whatever it is, is cloaked in nothing more than a vague hope modified by overtones of inevitable failure. Anderson has made clear his conviction that rebellion is not enough, but he is unable to go beyond that point either to the fulfillment that he seeks for his people, or to the constantly recurring tragedy that was so evident in the short stories.

This vagueness is not unexpected, however; rather, it parallels Anderson's own position. He had gone South after having completed *A Story Teller's Story,* not because he knew he would find any answers there but because he was continuing his search. In *Dark Laughter* Bruce Dudly is in the same situation, he returns to the small town in which he was born and by not anticipating the inroads of materialism, does not find what he sought. Anderson's artistic thoughtlessness lies in his own inability, thus far, to find purpose and direction after his personal rebellions. That he did not follow this novel with other fictional works but instead followed it with two more volumes of what, for want of a better word, must be called autobiography indicates his pressing need for answers to the questions he raised in his fiction and his continued inability to find them.

Dark Laughter had two important values for Anderson at this stage of his literary career: the obvious recognition that the modernist rebellion against puritanism, materialism, and conformity is not the answer but a beginning (the rejection of mere rejection); and less obvious, the recognition that shortcomings in man and society become ingrained under the pressure of materialism (you can't go home again). But at this point Anderson, working on *Tar: A Mid-West Childhood,* was seeking a vicarious return to an uncomplicated existence that he could not make.

Dark Laughter was Anderson's only work to approach the level of a best seller, paying him more than *$8000* during 1925. This money,

combined with several thousand dollars, from the serial rights to
Tar: A Midwest Childhood in the *Woman's Home Companion,* re-
moved temporarily the financial difficulties that were to continue to
plague him; it provided the opportunity for the last and most significant of his moves. In the hills of southwestern Virginia, which
he and Elizabeth had visited while he was working on *Tar,* he discovered Troutdale, Virginia, where:

> The mountain people are sweet. No books, little false education,
> real humbleness. It does so beat talking to pretentious half-artists.
> We may try to acquire a few acres and a cabin . . . . Everyone
> wants you to come in, to drink moonshine, to eat, to spend the
> night.

With the money from his successes he was able to afford more
than a few acres and a cabin; although he was committed to a late-
fall lecture tour, he made arrangements to buy Ripshin Farm near
Troutdale and start construction of a big stone house. Meanwhile,
back in New Orleans he postponed the final revisions of *Tar* long
enough to collect essays, sketches, and bits of memoirs from the past
few years to put them together under the title of *Sherwood Anderson's Notebook,* which was published in the spring of 1926. It appeared in the midst of a personal crisis. His brother Earl, who had
lived with him for a time in Elyria, turned up in New York after
13 years of silence, partially paralyzed, poor, and a failure in his
attempts to become an artist. Karl had been caring for him, but
Sherwood was eager to help. At the same time he was ashamed of
his success in the light of Earl's failure. Nevertheless, he insisted
that Earl come to the farm to recuperate and make it his home. At
this time, too, Anderson's son John was determined to be an artist,
and Anderson was trying to combine his own sympathy with the
boy's ambition with a proper sense of parental caution and prudence.
When *Sherwood Anderson's Notebook* was published, he was so busy
with family and farm that he paid little attention to the event. He
hoped, he commented, that it had ". . . a healthy, nice tone," but
the book can hardly be described that way. Instead it is the record
of the years of frustration, despair, and rejection from the time of
Poor White until he began to regain his equilibrium with the publication of *A Story Teller's Story.*

Sherwood Anderson's Notebook is more than a convenient ". . .
collection of magazine pieces written several years earlier," [2] as

---

[2] Irving Howe, *Sherwood Anderson* (New York, 1951), p. 208.

Irving Howe dismisses it. Unfortunately misinterpreted and ignored by critics, it provides insight into Anderson's thinking and attitudes during the period of wandering after he rejected the liberation, and it shows the development of the style he used with limited success in *Dark Laughter*. Also, in spite of the air of bitterness and pessimism that permeates the later pieces, the *Notebook* shows the turning point that led him to Troutdale, which he accepted as a counterpart of the simple, honest ways of late nineteenth-century Clyde, Ohio.

The collection is more than an artless and naive notebook or daybook containing the distilled wit and wisdom of the author. Actually, it is a loosely-chronological series of observations, impressions, and experiences, but it does not represent Anderson as he was when it was published; instead it shows him at his low point during which the stories of frustration and despair were written. Here one sees the state of mind behind the stories—a state that sees no hope for modern man as a group, as an individual, or as Sherwood Anderson, unappreciated and impoverished writer. He does not foresee the success of *Dark Laughter* as a best seller, the generally successful lecture tours, or the security of place that the farm was to provide.

Anderson's state of mind is best shown in three of the essays, "I'll Say We've Done Well," "Notes on Standardization," and "When the Writer Talks." The first, written in 1922, is a look at his native state of Ohio and in it, Anderson is bitter. Ohio, he says, has not realized its potential as a place where the individual could find a meaningful life; instead, it has become as dirty a place as it is possible to find. Anderson's irony becomes denunciation as he comments that Ohio cities ". . . can put themselves forward as being as ugly, as noisy, as dirty, and as careless . . . as any American cities anywhere." But his denunciation is not mere muckraking; it is bitter regret at what has occurred:

> . . . I claim we Ohio men have taken as lovely a land as ever lay outdoors and that we have, in our cities and towns, put the old stamp of ourselves on it for keeps.

But it was not easy, Anderson comments: "First we had to lick the poet out of our hearts and then we had to lick nature herself; but we did it."

In "Notes on Standardization," Anderson continues in this vein, examining the mass-produced culture of America until he sees no way out of the dirt around him, and he cries out, "Are our lives worth living? Is it living at all to spend all of our best years in helping to build cities larger . . . make more dirt and noise and indulge in an ever-increasingly louder talk of progress?" Nevertheless, more in hope than in conviction he continues on a lower pitch: "Or is there a quieter, more leisurely and altogether more charming way of life we might begin to live, here in America?" To this, there is no answer in the essay.

"When the Writer Talks" brings Anderson's personal problems into the picture. Not only is lecturing a necessary evil that takes him away from the writing he should be doing, but it poses new problems. Basically he feels that it is silly and degrading, and at the same time that it stimulates him, raising the old question of the dichotomous values that he finds in himself. On one hand, he says, " 'This lecturing business is so exciting and interesting. I love it.' " On the other, he feels that " 'This lecturing business is so terrible. It makes me feel so cheap.' "

"King Coal," like "Notes on Standardization," passes beyond regret and bitterness and points out the increasing need that Anderson feels for a sense of place and permanence in his life, the need that led him to buy the farm in Virginia: "If a man live in a street in a modern industrial town can he love that street? If a man does not love the little patch of ground on which his own house may stand can he in any sense love the street, the city, the state, the country of which it is a part?"

Beside this record of his despair, his frustration, and his need to identify himself with a place that will ease his growing despair, the book contains liberal samples of Anderson's newly acquired *Dark Laughter* style, in passages that suffer in comparison with the unpretentious prose of the earlier essays. In the intermittent "Notes Out of a Man's Life," comments interspersed between the essays that are the product of odd moments during and after the writing of *Dark Laughter*, Anderson employs the jerky, disjointed, impressionistic prose style that hinders and distorts the clear expression of his thought. Nevertheless, here too, the bitterness grows softer toward the end, as his personal problems become eased and Ripshin Farm comes closer to reality as a place in which he can find refuge from the harshness of America. The final sketch, that of a man who has rediscovered craftsmanship, is the reiteration of Anderson's belief that although the end of his search may be beyond his abilities to grasp, nevertheless, he can find a measure of satisfaction and fulfillment in the means.

Sherwood Anderson's Notebook remains as the last real expression of his doubts about his own place in modern America and about his inability to put into practice the only solutions he saw for the problems of modern society. The return to pride and satisfaction in work; to compassion, love, and understanding for other human beings; and to a state of innocence, even though it might at times be brutal, were fine theories. But he knew that in a modern, sophisticated society, talking about them was futile, even among those whom he had regarded as fellow revolutionaries. Although these were the only possible solutions that he could see, he realized that his talking, like his father's before him, could only be ignored or misinterpreted in a materialistic society.

The end of this book, like that of *A Story Teller's Story*, points toward a period of withdrawal from the public scene and a concentrated attempt to find meaning in life. Early in the summer of 1926, he and Elizabeth moved into the completed house on the farm near Troutdale, planning to remain there, where he hoped to find peace in a simple life. There he found the way of life that he depicted in *Tar* and that he had thought was gone:

> . . . a way of life that is outside the tone of most America just now. The machine has not penetrated deeply into the hills. Hand weaving is still being done. Grain is still cut with a cradle. You may see oxen on the hill roads and in the fields, and when a man dies his neighbors come to his house and build his coffin in the yard before his door . . . . The hills have, however, their own fools, their beautiful women, their liars, their over-sensitive and their easily-hurt ones.

Tar: A Midwest Childhood is the product of this new sense of discovery. Anderson makes it the record, not only of his own childhood, but of an America still possessed of much of the innocence, exuberance, wonder, and unconscious brutality of all childhood. It is his attempt to fuse past and present and to compile a portrait of a world in which it would be possible for man to practice the virtues that would lead him to fulfillment; it is the temporary world of the 1870s and 1880s in rural Ohio made permanent as a refuge for his dreams; and at the same time, it is his hope that such a place still exists in the hill country.

In *Tar*, Anderson is not attempting to provide either a real or an idealized portrait of an America that he would like to see return in fact. Rather, through his intuitive approach to understanding, he is trying to recapture the spirit of that earlier time with its code of inarticulated values, its assessment of the worth of the individual, as shown in his actions. Kindnesses shown to an insignificant boy or a pot of soup carried to a sick neighbor are more meaningful than all the millions of dollars poured into impersonal, standardized, and dehumanized charity.

On the jacket of the book is the comment that "It is, of course, autobiographical, as such a book would be bound to be, but it is not written as an autobiography." In actuality as well as in intent, *Tar* is another of the combinations of fact and fiction that have exasperated category-minded critics. In the foreword, Anderson states that his purpose in writing the book is his belief that "Like every other man and woman in the world I had always thought the story of my own childhood would be an absorbingly interesting one," but as he points out, his real reason is not quite that simple. If it were, the story as it had been told in *Windy McPherson's Son* and *A Story Teller's Story* might have been sufficient. But neither of these satisfied him because in both he had missed the "spirit of something" that he had been trying to catch. Now he was starting over, reinterpreting, in the hope that this time he might grasp that "something." His neglect of the facts is deliberately dismissed by him, with pretended naïveté, as a writer's fancy; but as both his letters and later *Memoirs* show, he was deadly serious in writing the book.

The reason for returning to his childhood as a background in *Tar* is made clear by what he had discovered in re-examining the cyclical structure of his life in *A Story Teller's Story*. In that book he saw the Clyde years as essentially good and meaningful in spite of occasional brutality. The early Chicago years he saw as meaningless in spite of his increased awareness of the worth of the individual. The army period was good; the following commercial years bad; the early writing years good and the later "literary" years bad. In *A Story Teller's Story* he rejected both the commercial and the "literary" years as bad. The early writing years he saw as a time of personal discovery impossible to recapture; and he found that the meaning of his Spanish-American War experience was much different from its appearance. The only place in his experience that seemed to him to contain absolute and meaningful social and personal values was the Clyde, Ohio, of his childhood and youth, and *Tar* is the re-creation in depth of that time and place.

The outline of *Tar* is almost identical with the autobiographical materials Anderson had used in both *Windy McPherson's Son* and *A Story Teller's Story*; but his presentation of these facts is a complete repudiation of the interpretation put on them in the former and an amplification of that in the latter. The most important new material that Anderson introduces is a dream of childhood and youth that had largely faded away under the impact of materialism in adulthood. The revelation of his dream points out what he is looking for in writing the book—a town, perfect in its pastoral simplicity, a town that he acknowledges could not possibly exist in fact. Whether the dream was actually a dream of his youth or whether Anderson imagined its existence as a frustrated adult does not matter. What does matter is his seeking in his imagination for a refuge where he could withdraw from the world.

The portrayals of both the father and the mother re-evolve from the point at which he left them in *A Story Teller's Story*. In the father, Anderson completes the portrayal of the mythological free adventurer-craftsman-storyteller, and solidifies his earlier tentative identification. The father tells tales of his real or imaginary adventures; he goes steadily downhill from craftsman to employee to wanderer; and he is just as disreputable as Windy McPherson, but here Anderson takes pride in the disreputableness which he identifies with his own; like his father, "Tar became a story teller but, if you will notice, it is the shiftless roving fellows who tell tales. Few tellers of tales are good citizens. They only pretend to be."

The portrayal of the mother has also become clarified in comparison to the earlier portrayals. No longer is she the patient, suffering, pitiable woman of *Windy McPherson's Son*. Although still inarticulate and remote, she is no longer tortured by her life as the wife of a wastrel; her evolution, begun in *Winesburg, Ohio* when she sought fulfillment vicariously, is now carried through to completion. Combining compassion, service, and intuitive understanding in the mysterious role of motherhood, she emerges as a woman fulfilled. As a result, she is no longer a person; she has become the symbol of female strength and innate wisdom on which Anderson will later build his hopes in *Perhaps Women*.

More important than these changing views of the parent images, however, are two aspects of the book that point out the "spirit of

something" that Anderson seeks. The first of these is Tar's introduction to an awareness of and reverence for life. In a manner that
is gradual, natural, and accepted in such an environment, Tar comes
to realize that, as diverse as the many facets of life are, they are
nevertheless, part of a whole. The sounds of rural life stirring in the
morning, the feel of a horse's tongue on his hand, and the attempt
to emulate animals by eating the grass are to him the earliest
manifestations of life. Later, these impressions are combined with
other discoveries: the potential threat of a newborn child; the sheer
enjoyment of spring grass after the winter; and, more vividly, the
sting of a bee and the increasing desire to know the wonder of a
girl's body. This growth of intuitive insight into the mystic nature
of life is epitomized in the sketch of the old woman who dies alone
in the woods, the best passage in the book. The boy ponders on the
meaning of her death, but as Anderson points out, only the adult
can look back and see that both the growth of the boy's awareness
and his bewilderment at the incident in the woods are part of a
whole and are to be valued equally. But the adult can know this
only after he has learned that society denies the ultimate unity of
life and death, nature and man.

Equally important to his adult recognition of the child's closeness
to truth is his reconsidered view of the town itself, a view that
produces the most nostalgic thing Anderson had yet written. Here
are the fertile countryside and the town's closeness to it; the give-
and-take of small-town raillery; early morning at the race track;
the quiet of a drive through the country; and the excitement of
Saturday night on Main Street. But this is merely background for
the recognition of the values that Tar had not accepted. The town
was a society in which dignity was accorded to the individual on
the basis of his character. Although Tar recognized this value instinctively, the imagined stigma attached to his father prevented
him from becoming a full participant in the town life, and in self-
defense he became a hustler as he accepted other values.

Albeit Anderson's portrait of the town is not one-sided. He ". . . is
no necromancer," as Maxwell Geismar[3] points out. Even in retro-
spect Anderson remembers that:

> Boys, Tar's own age, had secret vices. Some of the boys at the
> swimming hole did things, said things. When men grow older they

[3] Maxwell Geismar, *The Last of the Provincials* (Boston, 1949), p. 261.

grow sentimental about the old swimming hole. They remember only the pleasant things that happened. There is a trick of the mind that makes you forget the unpleasant. It's just as well. If you could see life clear and straight maybe you could not live.

Although Tar did not realize it then, evil did exist, along with the good, but it was human evil stemming from innocence rather than the inhumanity of materialism. Instead, he accepted the values of the new materialism as good, and with that he rushed into maturity, leaving innocence behind. Only much later, as Anderson points out, could he realize his loss.

As an attempt to capture the essence of the values that Anderson wanted America to accept in place of material standards, and that he sought for himself, the book is successful; but many factors combine to prevent its complete success as a work of literary art. The first of these is the repetitious nature of the material used, especially since it was written so soon after *A Story Teller's Story*. Critics complained that Anderson had exhausted his creative imagination at this point and was reduced to reusing the same material. In spite of the importance of this book as an interpretation of what Anderson was seeking in his own life, the criticism has some validity. Even the new materials, the new interpretations, and the interesting attempts to reconstruct a world view as seen through the eyes of a child are not enough to overcome the repetitiousness of the book. But when it is read apart from Anderson's other works of the time, its merits are obvious.

Structurally, the book is one of Anderson's best works, having none of the jarring structural weaknesses of his previous novels. The narrative is unified, but stylistic difficulties that he should have been able to remove occur frequently to mar the work. Not only are they obvious shortcomings, such as awkward sentences and grammatical weaknesses, but a more serious deficiency is his attempt to return to his *Winesburg* style as a child would write it. Consequently, the effect of the solid Midwestern style he had evolved is often lost, and a weak imitation of it predominates until it becomes too evident that he is an adult trying consciously to relive his childhood.

In spite of these two weaknesses the book is an important one in Anderson's career. It is a book he had to write at this point, as it is his most eloquent denial of the critical generalities that have surrounded his work. It certainly refutes the persistent myths that he was a naturalist or that he was revolting from the village, and it points out his true attitudes toward both life and the small town. More important, however, it comes as close to being a positive statement of Anderson's personal values as it was possible for him to write, up to this point.

The values he had found in his imaginative return to the Clyde, Ohio, of the late nineteenth century are the values that he sought to surround himself with in Troutdale, Virginia. As he concluded this long period of introspection, he had achieved identity and vindication and finally, a sense of permanence and refuge in a world increasingly hostile to his ideals.

This sense of security was not to last, however; already factors were combining to destroy it. Economic chaos was not far off and it would shake even the Virginia hills; his marriage had reached a peak of success and would soon begin to decline; and most important, the long period of introspection had done damage to the literary reputation he was just beginning to enjoy. He felt that the period was successful from his point of view; he had achieved satisfaction and had even made some money, but he was convinced that this period's writing was not as good as it should have been, and he was having difficulty with a new novel, *Talbot Whittingham*, which he finally abandoned after numerous false starts.

Even though it is understandable when viewed in the light of the personal and ideological crisis that he was undergoing, Anderson's creative abilities had declined during this period. That they had not disappeared altogether is shown in the many excellent passages in all his books of this period and in "Death in the Woods," which followed *Tar*. But the major works of the period are marred by stylistic difficulties that could have been eliminated easily if it were not for his increased tendency toward an experimentation that was actually imitation, and by the haste with which he wrote all the books.

In spite of his new sense of identification and his discovery of a place in which he could live, he had found no ultimate answers, and he was beginning to realize that he never would. A quick trip to Europe to arrange for foreign publication of *Winesburg, Ohio, A Story Teller's Story,* and *Sherwood Anderson's Notebook,* made him more determined than ever to make complete his withdrawal from the world. On his return to the farm he wrote to Paul Rosenfeld that "It helps being down here. I'm done with cities . . . I wanted to bury myself in the field and come up green." He was ready to use Ripshin Farm as a refuge from the world of literature as well, he wrote Rosenfeld, because:

> I went to Paris and found myself close to famous. That's just plain sickening. God knows, I hope you escape it. It's sheer nonsense without a spark of meaning.

In his efforts to forget that "nonsense" he buried himself in enjoyment of the countryside, he sought to gather his children and his old friends around him, and he worked at a new volume of verse, *A New Testament.* At this point Anderson was tired, and it would take a long time for him to regain the confidence that he almost had within his grasp. He had rationalized his problems and he had returned to an older way of life, but he still had to learn to live it.

6

THE TOWNSMAN

DURING the late twenties and early thirties, Anderson withdrew almost entirely both from literary work and from the literary scene. Not only did his literary reputation and output decline, but he was afraid that his career was over, despite the fact that he knew "Death in the Woods" was one of his best stories. During the few weeks in Paris in January 1927, he was at his low point:

> Everything I have written seems dead stuff. . . . I work on a novel for a week, then throw it away. I write a short story. It seems nothing. . . . I can see nothing I am doing as really worth presenting.

At the same time, however, his old illogical optimism reasserted itself:

> Well, I'm too old a bird to think it is all necessarily final for me. I have waded through other long swamps. . . . I may right myself like an old ship.

After his return to America the despair continued:

> Long days nothing to do. "Write, man." But what shall I write? I am sitting on a hill in the country or walking in the streets of a town. I am in despair, such despair. . . .

This mood was to continue until he made another decision following his withdrawal to Virginia. He had to give up the idea of trying to earn his living by writing. He considered returning to the city to find a job, but rejected the idea when the opportunity came to buy the two weekly newspapers in nearby Marion—*Smyth County News*, Republican, and *Marion Democrat*, Democratic. A loan from a wealthy admirer, Burton Emmet, made the purchase possible. In late 1927 he became a country editor, a role that absorbed his energies and allowed him to return to close association with his people.

He celebrated the decision to become a townsman in *A New*

Testament, a collection of verse and verse prose which he published in 1927. This volume has much in common with *Mid-American Chants* in that it, like the earlier collection, marks the end of one phase of Anderson's life and writing career and the beginning of another, and it bears the same relationship to Anderson's prose style of the late 1920s, in which he was beginning to abandon his Joycean experiments, as *Mid-American Chants* bore to the solid prose of *Winesburg, Ohio.* Like the earlier volume of verse, *A New Testament* marks a stylistic as well as a personal change.

Alternated with the notes of celebration and affirmation that predominate the volume are shadows and echoes of the fears that had plagued Anderson during most of the 1920s, the same shadows of brutality and harshness that drift into *Tar.* But essentially *A New Testament* is, like *Tar,* a reaffirmation of what Anderson had long believed, and it heralds his full acceptance of his role as townsman. Its over-all tone is one of joy and release, and although it is not a serious effort at poetry, occasional flashes of insight and frequent pleasing phrases make it often rewarding. It is Anderson indulging himself, looking on the remote past fondly and the immediate past fearfully; acknowledging the harshness of the present; and looking forward to an uncomplicated future in an uncomplicated environment.

In "Testament," one of the earlier verses, he sets the tone of optimism and affirmation. He is, he says, writing a testament ". . . of one who would be a priest"; yet he can only ". . . stumble into the pathway of truth. . . . I smell the footsteps of truth but I do not walk in the footsteps." He knows what he is seeking, but he does not know how to find it except through his old intuitive empathy: "It is when you are torn from your moorings and drift like a rudderless ship that I am able to come near to you." He had been drifting aimlessly for most of his life, and he understands it in others.

"Song Number Three" celebrates his role as a storyteller freed from the restraints of convention, and "Song Number Four" carries on this celebration as it emphasizes the optimism of his new role as a townsman. In verses such as "Hunger" he sees life as promising, and in "Death" he finds a new sense of identity with the world and with others. In "Ambition," however, he returns to his quandary:

> I am one who has walked out of a tall building into the streets of a city and over plains into a forest that fringes a river. My notion

is one of escape. I can no longer bear the life led in my father's house. I am a child and cannot escape out of my childhood. There is a door through which I cannot enter, a wall I cannot climb. The idea of escape long ago attacked the seat of my reason.

From this rejection, wandering, and searching has come a new discovery:

I have remade the land of my fathers.
I have come out of my house to remake the land.
I have made a flatplace with the palms of my hands.

This is the discovery that Anderson focuses on in most of the volume: the sense of identity and the sense of belonging that he had sought in reinterpreting his past. The shorter pieces like "A Persistent Lover" and "The Visit in the Morning" reaffirm his old faith in the goodness of people reaching out to understand each other.

"The Dumb Man" from *The Triumph of the Egg* provides a jarring backward glance that tempers the optimism of these short pieces, but Anderson returns again to affirmation and celebration. Only once, however, does he look away from his newly-discovered role and place. In this verse, "A Young Jew," he recoils in horror from its portrayal of the destruction of human individuality. This mood continues in "The Story Teller," until his new optimism reasserts itself.

The last verses are an affirmation of his beliefs. "Young Man Filled with Power" is a strange verse for Anderson at this stage of his life, yet it represents the youthful strength and confidence that surged over him as he learned to understand his past. "Two Glad Men" carries this feeling of strength to the threshold of sheer joy; while the final verse, "A Man and Two Women Facing the Sea," represents Anderson's paradoxical position at the time. The imponderables, fears, and misunderstandings of the past have been overcome, but their shadows are still with him; and although he has found the direction he must follow in the future, he is impatient at his slowness.

As a creative work, *A New Testament* is unimportant in the Anderson canon. The volume, as verse, cannot stand on its own merits; the verses do not convey emotions that can be vicariously experienced; and they are repetitious and awkward. The book does show that Anderson has decided to abandon the Joycean experimental prose and structural patterns that had marred *Dark Laugh-ter,* and has returned to his Midwestern idioms and rhythms; and just as *Mid-American Chants* had celebrated the emergence of Anderson the conscious literary artist, this volume marks the emergence of Anderson the townsman.

Anderson had not expected the book to be successful, and he was not surprised at its critical reception. ". . . the *Testament* has brought down a furor on my head," he wrote. "My death as a writer is being tolled up and down the literary press. The crapehangers have all been busy. Well, I have been thrown that before. It does not matter much." What did matter was his new role as townsman-editor of Marion, Virginia. The purchase of the papers had given him a new interest and a new purpose in life. During his few years as editor and townsman he was a happy man. Summing up his new life, he wrote:

> Now I am getting up in the morning at six and am at my desk at eight. I do everything. A man wants a little handbill got up for the sale of steers. I write it for him. An old mossback farmer comes in and spends an hour trying to get me to knock off 25 cents on the subscription price of his paper. I enjoy it all and in the moments I catch am writing again. That is what a man lives for.

During the fall and winter of 1927, and all of 1928, the papers and the life of the town occupied almost all of Anderson's attention and energy. Never having been seriously interested in practical politics, Anderson farmed out the political editorials to local politicians, but the life and news of the town he reserved as his responsibility. Creative work became an avocation, so that he was truly the country editor. Civic projects and needs, ranging from the jail to the band, "Henry Mencken Park" (a rubbish-strewn lot that he wanted to beautify), and a lending library were sponsored by his editorial columns. News items were mixtures of fact, conjecture, and imagination that had no relation to textbook maxims of journalism but were closely related to the life in the town and the surrounding hill country. The result was country journalism, free from the pressures imposed by the profit system. His approach was successful. Not only did Anderson get ". . . 150 new subscribers in six weeks without asking anyone," but many of the articles were reprinted in national magazines; especially in *Vanity Fair,* and in early 1929 he was able to combine much of the best of the material into a book, *Hello Towns!*

During these months of devotion to the papers, Anderson entered into the life of Marion as completely as "Jobby" Anderson had in Clyde, Ohio, 30 years before. He solicited advertisements, attended meetings of clubs and the town council, covered trials, and spent a good deal of time gossiping on the steps of the courthouse. In all that time he was storing up ideas, impressions, and information, as he had done in Clyde, gathering the raw material for his future work, and drawing closer to the townspeople. At the same time, however, he knew that he could never fully belong to the life of the town, as he had never fully belonged in Clyde, and his sense of isolation was evident in occasional editorials.

Anderson was worried about his inability to carry on sustained creative work other than that for the papers. He started several new things and then abruptly abandoned them, unable to force himself to continue. Then, too, he disliked the condescension with which several of his friends regarded his new career. There was nothing phoney about it, he asserted in one testy letter; he was beginning to live out of himself again through knowing, loving, and enjoying natural and honest people.

During the months as country editor, his third marriage began to deteriorate, and early in 1929, he and Elizabeth separated; she going to California and he becoming restless as his inability to do sustained creative work continued. As in the case of his previous marriages, this one had been based on a time of his life that had passed, and Anderson, the country editor and former prominent writer, was not the man Elizabeth had married five years ago. In Virginia, Elizabeth had tried to pretend that his creative impulse was still strong; she saw the farm as a literary salon, and she was unsympathetic with his increased frustration at his inability to do any sustained writing. Anderson could not tolerate those attitudes.

After this break, Anderson left the papers in charge of his son Robert and began to wander—to Florida, to Chicago, and then back to the farm. His prime interest in these months was in putting together *Hello Towns!*, published in the fall of 1929, and in concentrating on creative work; the only tangible results of which were three short books, *Nearer the Grass Roots, Alice and The Lost Novel*, and *The American County Fair*.

Hello Towns! takes up where he had left off in *A New Testament*; it, too, is a testament of belief in his rediscovery of a way of life and a scale of values he thought had disappeared. Essentially it records that rediscovery, reaffirms his belief in the intrinsic worth of uncomplicated human life, and provides the key to the problems that had prevented his doing sustained creative work during the previous two years.

The rediscovery is shown in the relation between the impressionistic world of Tar Moorehead and the factual world of the country editor. Here the events that had so impressed a small-town boy— ". . . births and deaths, what the churches are doing . . . . Who gets hurt during the fall threshing or shoots somebody for getting gay with his wife . . . ."—are transposed into the efforts of the country editor ". . . to give expression to the joys and sorrows, the political fights, all of the everyday life of a very typical American community." That Marion was not a typical American community of the 1920s did not occur to Anderson; it was typical of America as he wanted it to be.

Reaffirmation of his belief in the intrinsic worth of human life is evident as Anderson moves beyond reportorial journalism and shows that the factual material he is dealing with is significant in its own right. Here in the news items describing the life of the town he shows the core of his beliefs: the worth and dignity of the individual, the enduring goodness inherent in living close to others, and the satisfaction inherent in a good job well done. *Hello Towns!* is complete affirmation of his long series of rejection of the values he felt were false in American life.

The reason for his inability to carry through creative projects is evident in the volume. During these months, his life had been devoted to rediscovering the essence of America, and he was becoming familiar with the material that would form the foundation for his work in the 1930s—work as different from that of the previous few years as *Winesburg, Ohio* was from *Marching Men*. During the next few years he was to record the impact of industrialism on the individual Southerner, just as he had attempted to do for the Midwesterner in *Poor White,* and he was beginning to know those Southern townsmen just as he had come to understand the townsmen in Clyde, Ohio, before giving them significance in *Winesburg*. *Hello Towns!* shows that he had gained insight into the lives of the people with whom he now identified himself.

In the foreword Anderson explains the background, or purpose, of the work. In it he records briefly how and why he had turned to country journalism: ". . . there is no place for the artist in American

Courtesy of The Newberry Library

SHERWOOD ANDERSON IN HIS PRESSROOM (JANUARY 1941)

life," he says. Writing should not be an occupation but a spontaneous thing; however, in America one must have an occupation, so he had drifted aimlessly, finally resolving to be a countryman. After buying his farm, he had been idle until he bought the newspapers, finding through them a sense of purpose and belonging to his rural environment. This presentation of what is ostensibly a factual account is oversimplified and dramatized to the extent that it, too, has become part of the Anderson myth, but it does convey the spirit of what Anderson had done in Virginia: he had found a place in America where he belonged.

Hello Towns! is organized to represent a year in the life of the country editor, from November to the following October; and in it, Anderson has compiled a cross section of the life of the small town in pieces ranging from accounts of shooting scrapes to editorials on "The New Frankness," on Van Gogh, on the role and purpose of the town band, on the solid virtues of American life, on the need for remodeling the town jail. Throughout the factual accounts of events that occur in the town, the apparent trivia that make up the town's gossip, Anderson focuses on significances; he reports events as manifestations of the meaning of life rather than as isolated segments of fact included to edify the idly curious or to flatter the participants. In so doing, he has rejected the usual journalistic techniques and has applied craftsmanship to the raw material of news, giving it meaning by writing to his readers as participants in the human experience. The selection of a few paragraphs at random from almost any of his news stories is sufficient to illustrate this approach. For example, under the heading "At Chilhowie, William McVey 15 Kills His Cousin Paul McVey 17," Anderson incorporates his concept of what journalism can be:

> The quiet and peace of an unusually beautiful Sunday was broken by a shocking killing at Chilhowie. William McVey, son of Andy McVey, a farmer living near Chilhowie, stabbed and killed his cousin, Paul McVey, a son of Harrison McVey, another farmer and the brother of Andy McVey.
>
> The cutting was done with a pocket knife and the boy who did the cutting is but fifteen. His dead cousin was seventeen.
>
> Our correspondent says the boys had been playmates for a long time. The two farms were near each other. The boys had been trapping and got into a quarrel over the ownership of a steel trap. They became inflamed by passion and a fight started. In the fight

the younger boy drew his pocket knife and stabbed his cousin in the neck. The jugular vein was cut and the boy died within the hour. William McVey was brought to Marion and lodged in the jail here.

Here is the essence of Anderson as journalist, as townsman, as writer. First of all, the event is not treated as news but as human tragedy; the tone is regretful and compassionate. There is no indignation or condemnation; instead, there is a recognition that such things happen because people are human, and behind the event are the implications of all that humanity entails. Here, too, the style Anderson employs is designed to engender in his readers the empathy he feels. This is not mere journalism; it is an attempt to convey human feeling, and in so doing, Anderson has presented in microcosm the tragedy inherent in human life as pointedly as he had in many of his short stories.

In the editorial writings, Anderson presents a picture of himself in his new role. He is mentor, spokesman, booster, participant in the life of the town. The editorial column becomes for him a pulpit, a lectern, and a cracker barrel, and on occasion, a confessional. In "Group Feeling" it becomes the confessional, as he admits the inadequacy he has always felt in the company of others; in "Here Comes the Band" he is a booster of one of the town's sources of pride; in "Gil Stephenson" he preaches the doctrine of craftsmanship; in "Hello Towns!" and in "Aftermath" he draws close to the cracker barrel and gives his candid appraisal of the world, the town, and the events that keep both from stagnation.

At first glance *Hello Towns!* may seem to be a collection of news items, sketches, random thoughts, jottings, and ideas put together in a hit-or-miss fashion reminiscent of a shotgun blast; but it is not. It is one of Anderson's most carefully constructed books, even though its material is much more diverse than anything he had previously attempted. The device of using a month-by-month approach ties it together as well as could be expected. It is not unified, since the events and relationships that make up a town's life are diverse and spontaneous. Tragedy, humor, pathos, trivia—none of it significant except in its relationship to the lives involved—are the materials of a town's life, and it is this material that Anderson put together to make this book.

Here is the record of a man who looks at the town around him

and finds it worthwhile and meaningful. In the same manner, he
has found meaning in the role he is playing in that town. That this
has nothing to do with journalism he is well aware: "I cannot be a
slave to the papers. I shall let my fancy loose . . . . There are
stories here . . . . There will be this life of the town and my own
life outside. There is the life of the fancy too." In setting forth the
philosophy of his new venture, he reiterates at the same time that
his new life and role have not made him forget his larger role as a
writer. As the book progresses, his attention is drawn more frequently to affairs of the outside world, he is increasingly preoccupied
with the problem of the artist in society, and he further injects fancy
into journalism as he moves back into the role of writer.

In venturing out of the small-town world to go to Washington to
interview Herbert Hoover, Secretary of Commerce under Coolidge,
he voices a vague discontent: "We who live in country towns miss
certain things. The radio and the phonograph can bring us music by
the best orchestras . . . we can hear speakers talk, but there are
things we cannot get . . . ." In his impressions of Hoover, he shows
a new awareness of the sense of the times outside the town, as well
as an insight into what both Hoover and his age needed.

> They [the industrialists] have raised this **Mr. Hoover** up out of
> the ranks of men as perhaps the finest Republican example of man-
> hood and ability in present-day American political and industrial life.
> He is, apparently, a man very sure of himself. His career has been
> a notable one. From a small beginning he has risen steadily in power.
> There has never been any check. I felt, looking at him, that he has
> never known failure.
>
> It is too bad never to have known that. Never to have known
> miserable nights of remorse, feeling the world too big and strange
> and difficult for you.

This moment of insight is not prophetic of Hoover's presidency,
of course, but it does indicate that Anderson is coming to a new and
valid understanding of his time, made possible only because, for the
first time, he felt a solid foundation of belonging. As he concludes
the essay, he points this out:

> I had tried to be smart and had not been smart. I had got myself
> into a false position. What happens to the age in which a man lives
> is like the Mississippi, a thing in nature. It is no good quarreling
> with the age in which you live.

In such pieces as "Conversing with Authors," "Just Walking," "The Winter's Trade," and "In New York," Anderson shows his continued concern with the problems of the artist in society; but here, too, his point of view has altered perceptibly from that in *A Story Teller's Story* and *The Modern Writer*. Formerly, he had been critical—he had felt that the serious artist should have more attention, understanding, and financial support. Here his point of view has shifted, as he attempts to explain the artist and to plead for understanding of him. Beneath the fun that Anderson pokes at himself, as he suggests segregation for all authors, it is evident that he realized that the intimacy shared between him and the town was primarily on the surface. In spite of his eagerness to belong, there were too many reasons why he could not; the townsmen were aware that he was part of a larger world of which they were ignorant, and he himself could not forget it.

Examples abound of his injection of artistic fancy into journalism. Not only has he introduced more or less stock characters—Buck Fever and Hannah Stoots—in humorous, semisatirical bits, but he has incorporated sketches such as "A Mountain Dance," "Small Town Notes," and "A Criminal's Christmas," which are as true in their insight into the nature of rural life as any of his news columns. "A Mountain Dance" depicts the insistent forces that carry human life spontaneously through its cycle. "Small Town Notes" is a simple, direct, and compassionate portrayal of two men: one dreamed futilely about being a baseball player; the other used his wife's objections as an excuse for his inability to do things that men were expected to do. Either sketch might have been the nucleus of another *Winesburg* story.

Through the unfolding months and the changing seasons that the book portrays, one is aware of the cycle of small-town life as in none of Anderson's other works, not even in *Tar*, where he had tried to create such a world out of his memory and imagination. Here, however, out of fact and fancy, observation and interpretation, he presents the ebb and flow of a town's life as a montage of sight, sound, and feeling. It is a picture of life that Anderson feels is real, honest, and understandable.

Anderson concludes *Hello Towns!* with an answer to the question "Will You Sell Your Newspapers?" His reply is indirect but entirely negative. Here, he says, in this place and in this town he has found that he belongs: "Yesterday I drove my car down a street of our town I had never been on before. I did not know the street was there. "Men hailed me. Women and children were sitting on doorsteps. 'It is our editor.' . . . I have a place in this community. How difficult to feel that in the city." Later he says, "A man has to work. He cannot be just a teller of old tales. He has to find somewhere a place into which he fits." A direct answer to the question is unnecessary.

As Anderson concluded *Hello Towns!* he felt some of his old confidence returning. He saw it as ". . . a damn good book . . . one of the best I ever did . . . . It's a real picture of life—fragmentary as I have been lately, but real . . . ." In this case his judgment, in spite of his enthusiasm, was sound. *Hello Towns!* is a good book of its type. It shows the potentialities inherent in journalism when it can afford to reject commercialism. It is real because it has been drawn from life; the people and situations it describes are the material of which human life is made. It is fragmentary because the material was not assimilated and digested, as it must be in fiction. The book is an affirmation of his belief in the material he had incorporated, even though he was eager to use the material in fiction, he did not know how to go about it.

Following *Hello Towns!* he published three short works, each in a limited edition. These three combined to bridge the gap between Anderson the country editor and Anderson the writer, who is very much aware that the town is not a refuge but a part of the world. The three works restate the values he has affirmed in *Hello Towns!* and, at the same time, they point out the direction his thinking and his work would take during the last ten years of his life.

The first of these works is *Nearer the Grass Roots*. It contains two short essays which are almost completely ignored even by Anderson scholars, but it occupies a key position in any attempt to understand the emergence of Anderson's role as townsman-philosopher, a role he assumed as the novelty of small-town journalism wore off and he decided that he could not cut himself off from the world in which he lived.

The first essay is an autobiographical sketch including in abbreviated form much of the material that Anderson had used in his earlier works; but in the last half of the essay he reveals what may be the reason for the difficulty he is encountering in resuming his creative work after his long period of introspection: "I was associating altogether too much with one Sherwood Anderson. I never grew so tired of a man in my life." He points out the values he has found in his new life: ". . . . It is the most fun of anything I have ever done in my life," and, of most importance to him:

> . . . there is the tremendous advantage of being in close and constant touch with every phase of life in an American community every day of the year. What could any writer ask more enticing than that?

The second of the two essays is "Elizabethton, An Account of a Journey." In this essay, Anderson points out the direction that much of his future work and interests would take. Elizabethton, Tennessee, was one of the new Southern cities whose growth was a result of the twentieth-century industrial revolution in the South. It had abundant water power, cheap labor, and some of the largest rayon mills in the country, and "It has been held up as representing the industrialist's finest and latest achievement in building an industrial town." Elizabethton was also the home of low wages, long hours, insecurity, and all the other evils of industrialism, including the dehumanizing aspects that Anderson had protested for so long. When the textile workers went out on strike, Anderson drove over from Marion for the story. What he saw as an observer was one of the factors that led him back into the world he could no longer ignore.

This essay is a series of impressions and includes pictures that still reflect the old Anderson, as well as those that foreshadow much of his future work. The impressions reflect the former state, but regret has replaced indignation:

> Here is a town not more than five years old. Already the buildings have that half-decrepit worn-out look that makes so many American towns such disheartening places. There is a sense of cheapness, hurry, no care for the buildings in which men and women are to work.

Here is Anderson's first direct contact with the machine since *Poor White,* and he still regards it with disapproval. In *Poor White* he had asserted that the machine had been accepted because it would result in good. At the same time, however, he saw it as an entity in itself, the product of man's inventive genius, and, neither good nor bad except as man directs it. He restates this belief, and the old bitterness flashes as he comments, "There is always the old question —to make men rise in nobility to the nobility of the machines." This has not yet happened in Elizabethton, he reflects. However, as the new union gives dignity and recognition to the workers and they find a new sense of belonging and of purpose, Anderson sees that there is a possibility that the machines may yet be used for the right ends.

Coupled with this are observations of the thin, too-young girls who lie about their ages to take jobs in the mills. This facet of industrialism had escaped him in his earlier fight against the giant; now his old indignation rises at the thought that the girls have no choice but to lie. Just before Anderson leaves Elizabethton, he notices a shoddy monument in the town square. "How I would have liked to see one of those delicately-featured, hard-bodied little mountain girls, done in stone by some real artist standing up there," he reflects.

The second of the short works is *Alice and The Lost Novel*. It contains two short pieces, both previously published in periodicals. The first of these, "Alice," is a brief attempt to define the beauty of a woman, an inner beauty that is seen as an ability to give of herself and to project understanding and trust to the men around her. Anderson personifies in Alice, the same intuitive wisdom and feeling that he found in his mother, and that Sam McPherson and Tar Moorhead had found in theirs. Here, however, Anderson has eliminated the dream quality that surrounded his earlier portrayals. Alice is an East Tennessee mountain girl grown into a woman of the world rather than the earlier Midwestern wife-mother, but the quality of understanding is the same; Anderson is feeling his way toward his monument to the mill girl and to women, and this is one of his tentative sketches.

The other piece, "The Lost Novel," is another attempt at a definition of something to which he had given much thought: the mystic qualities of the creative experience that occurs not in the artist's hands, or as a result of his materials, but in his mind and emotions. To him, the resulting work is only the tangible symbol of the act of creation, and it is less important than the act itself, which only the artist can experience.

In this short work, Anderson has also bridged the gap between past and present both in his life and in his work, just as he had in *Nearer the Grass Roots*. In it he has written one of his most pleasant works, embodying all the techniques of Midwestern storytelling, seeing connections where none are apparent, and finally making them clear as he rambles genially rather than blunders determinedly to his point. At the same time he provides sketches that are graphic in their insight.

The third of this series of short books was *The American County Fair,* published in 1930. This is Anderson at his Midwestern best in a sketch that combines his wealth of feeling for the smooth movement of the race horse with his love of the rural countryside and the uncontaminated past. Impressionistic rather than consciously descriptive, the sketch embodies Anderson's attempt to recapture and convey the sight, the sound, the flavor, and above all, the feeling of that exciting and typically rural aspect of American life. *The American County Fair* is another of Anderson's testaments. It is much more deeply felt and spontaneous than his efforts to recapture the feeling in verse, and it is more valuable and lasting because he is not consciously poetic. Rather, he is striving to convey feeling and to describe it at the same time, as he had learned to do for the newspapers. Anderson is well aware that this interlude of the fair is a passing thing, a fancy rather than a fact, however, and he concludes with the realization that even the beauty of the race horse is fleeting.

Between 1926 and 1931, Anderson's creative ability was not dead, as some of his critics maintain, and as he himself feared. Although *A New Testament* is not of high caliber and his work had decreased quantitatively, nevertheless his use of the new material from his experiences in the South shows that his ability to perceive meaning intuitively and to communicate it effectively was still very much alive. But in the works that he abandoned during those years, it is evident that he was wrongly trying to use material from the period of *Many Marriages* and *Dark Laughter* rather than of his rediscovery of intrinsic human values.

During most of 1929, he worked on a novel first called *No Love,* later *No God* and *Sacred Service,* and finally *Beyond Desire,* but it had nothing to do with the later novel entitled *Beyond Desire.* Desperately trying to prove that he was not a has-been and trying to regain the critical and financial success that he had had with *Dark Laughter,* he revived its approach and technique. The novel as he conceived it was to be ". . . the story of a man having his roots in the pre-War life, accepting the present-day post-War life"—a man who was in love with a girl who was ". . . the young female kid of today. She has had sex experience and will have more, when she wants it." But the novel would not crystallize because it was a lie;

he knew it, although he could not yet force himself to admit it. In December 1929, he wrote his publisher, Horace Liveright:

> I think you know . . . that I have to have this book right, not only on account of its chances of success, but also because of myself. I want to whip out of me this sense of defeat I have had . . . . All I can say is that I will do nothing else . . . .

Two weeks later, however, after a meandering trip from Chicago to Florida, he knew that he had to admit the truth, both to himself and to Liveright:

> I never will write that novel now. The truth is I have been forcing my pace on it all the time.
>
> I'm going to fool around down here for a month or two and then go up into North Carolina and hang around there. The novel went wrong because I never was honest-to-God behind it. There were some gaudy chapters, but she didn't move . . .
>
> I've got an interest, though, and I'm going to go to it, though I'm not going to make promises about delivery. It is working people in the mills, particularly the working people, the poor whites, in the mills in the South. I'm going to build my novel around a little poor white mill girl, what happens to her coming to town, in a strike, etc. It's living stuff whether it will sell or not.

With this he began another period of wandering, but this time it was purposeful. Separated from his wife Elizabeth, with the newspapers in the hands of his son Robert, he was free to follow his new direction, wherever it might lead. He schemed to free himself of Ripshin Farm by turning it into a club. Fortunately the plan was unsuccessful, because the farm was to be a base of operations and a place in which to gain perspective during the remaining years of his life. At this time, however, he was beginning his last search, and he was attempting to free himself from any ties that might hinder it.

In the world that he was re-entering, the stock market crash had already occurred, and Coolidge prosperity was turning into Hoover Depression. Much of his future attention was to be directed toward finding a cure for that symptom of economic illness, as well as its causes. Part of this search was encouraged and directed by a young woman from Marion, Eleanor Copenhaver, who, as a social worker for the YWCA, was devoted to helping the mill girls of the South. Anderson and Elizabeth were divorced early in 1932, and he be-

gan to see a great deal of Miss Copenhaver. Their friendship soon
became love, but they did not marry until July 1933. In the meanwhile, they often traveled together through the mill towns of the
South, Eleanor in her official capacity and as a guide, and Anderson
as observer, as sympathizer, and as active participant in the effort to
bring dignity to the lives of Southern workers.

At this point Anderson was ready to work again. His writing was
slower than it had been in the past as he felt his way into what he
saw as a new, true novel, and his optimism was tempered by his
creative difficulties as well as the grimness of the world he was re-
entering, and by the subject matter of the new novel. He had few
illusions about his chances for success either in his work or in solving
the country's problems, but he was ready to try.

7

VENTURES INTO THE WORLD

D URING 1930 and 1931, when Sherwood Anderson began venturing into the world again, he was interested primarily in the impact of industrialism on the people of the New South. The Depression had not yet become intense in that area, but the period was marked by a long series of rebellions by the textile workers against the domination of the mills and the mill towns. As a newspaperman, as a compassionate human being, and as one who had long struggled against industrialism, he was disturbed by these social upheavals.

His writing during these years was concerned with the problem of the industrial impact and the search for an answer to it. Like many intellectuals of the time, he turned to communism as a possible answer. However, stung too many times by a too rapid commitment, he was cautious, but his brief flirtation has often been misconstrued. In November 1930, he wrote, "I am not so sure . . . that we want Socialism and certainly not wholesale Communism." He did want a closer look at both, however.

During the winter of 1930–1931, he actively supported the unsuccessful Danville, Virginia, textile strike. As a result, his involvement in the struggles became personal rather than objective. "Cotton Mill," "Danville, Virginia," and other essays, all concerned with the relationship between man and machine, appeared in *Scribners* and *New Republic*. Early in 1931, he began to compile the essays into a book in which he planned to take his readers with him into the factories.

This new book, *Perhaps Women,* was published in 1931 while Anderson was putting together a series of lectures to earn some money. Composed of the free verse, essays, sketches, and random thoughts that resulted from his trips through the industrial South, *Perhaps Women* deals with the wonder and fear with which he regards the machines, at the same time expressing a growing conviction that modern man is losing his manhood to the machines. As the title implies, Anderson feels that whatever hope remains for man in the factories lies in women, who are the real sources of strength in an industrial society.

The first piece, "Machine Song," attempts to convey the seductive qualities of an age that does so much, so easily; its repetitive style is lulling until suddenly Anderson points out that one must give up his individuality in order to belong to the new order. In "Lift Up Thine Eyes" he epitomizes the assembly-line techniques that conspire against the humanness of the workers. The title mocks the reverence demanded by the directors of the new age. "Loom Dance," too, conveys the wonder of the machines, but goes on to describe the momentary loom-induced madness of the workers who revolt but cannot stop the cloth-making process.

The essays "It is a Woman's Age" and "Perhaps Women" combine to show the result of this process by which man is dehumanized, and what Anderson feels is the only remaining hope for man. In the former he maintains that dignity and ability have been taken from men and given to the machines, so that the traditional strengths of maleness have been eliminated. The women coming into the factories in increasing numbers recognize this loss and tend to shun the men as lovers and mates. Women, he says, always rule in a factual age; as a result, they are destined to rule in this one.

In the essays Anderson maintains that the machine has come to dominate much of the South, having conquered, destroyed, or seduced those who would stand against it; it has come to have a life of its own, tolerating the men and women who serve it because they are its slaves. At the same time, Anderson ironically points out that the machine, by contributing to ever-increasing overproduction, is bringing about the economic destruction of its age.

The essay "Perhaps Women" emphasizes this point, using as a basis for its evidence Anderson's observations in the factories. He sees the increasing technological unemployment resulting from increased use of automatic machinery, and the obvious confusion resulting among the workers. He sees the result of all this to be a process of degeneration that has demoralized both the workers and the middle classes to the point where all of society has lost its sense of personal worth to the impersonal machines.

"Night in a Mill Town," "Ghosts," and "Entering the Mill at Night" explore the hidden fear of the machine shown by millowners, supervisors, and workers alike. At the same time Anderson notes ᵗthat each one seeks and accepts his place in the hierarchical system of industrialism. Without using the term, he is talking about the concept of the organization man, which America finally discovered more than 25 years later. In mill-owned towns in the South, he sees the organization's domination of society, in that even the schools and churches are built, and the teachers and preachers paid by the factories. The result is control of the means of expressing opinion and the disenfranchisement of the residents through political manipulations, a consequence Anderson finds terrifying. He sees no escape except through his faith in the power of women to save men from the effects of their own folly, and he asks women to accept the responsibility to do so.

Men, he says, have been seduced and conquered by the vicarious power they derive from the machine; women have not because their fulfillment and function are internal. Only they can make the machine a servant instead of a master. In a vivid sketch at the end of the book he points out that the women are aware of the emasculation of their men. In a moment of relaxation in the mills the women are making fun of the men. They often do, he is told.

If Anderson's solution to the problems of industrialism seems naive and romantic, too steeped in the mysticism with which he approached women in his work, nevertheless, there is much validity in both his observation and interpretation of the life in the mills. He foresaw at that time industrial problems growing out of automation that are just now beginning to be felt. What he did not foresee in his study of the mills was the inevitable seduction of the women by the combination of mass production and mass advertising. But he was to see that in writing *Kit Brandon*.

As a collection of journalistic pieces, *Perhaps Women* is not as effective as *Hello Towns!* because of the nature of the material and the writing techniques he employed. In *Hello Towns!* he was concerned with human life, and his interest and compassion dominate the individual pieces; here, in spite of Anderson's fear and awe of the machines, he is unable to give them an air of significance, and the essays are often lifeless in comparison.

Because machines dominate the essays, Anderson attempts to convey their motion in his style. Unfortunately, in order to do so, he has often resorted to the jerky rhythmic pattern he had used in *Dark Laughter*. Instead of being a stylistic reproduction of the smooth motion of machines fed by machine-like men, the style seems to be a grotesque caricature of machine activity. His usually satisfactory Midwest rhythms would not have been adequate for the effect he wanted to create, but the disjointed, unrhythmical structures he has employed is not adequate either.

In *Perhaps Women,* the country editor seems at times to have almost disappeared, and flashes of Anderson's old bitterness and indignation occur. However, he is restrained for the most part, and although he registers concern, he knows that he himself is secure. Nevertheless he fears what the machine may do, even in his retreat of Marion, Virginia, and he knows that some of his fellow townsmen have already been seduced by its appeal. To his future mother-in-law, Laura Lou Copenhaver, he made his feelings clear:

> There you have Marion, a lovely little town really. And how quickly the citizens would rush forward to bring there some dirty factory, making cheap goods of some kind, pouring more cheap, shoddy goods out into the world. And they would call that Love of Their Town. A bit more money brought to a few, the rest degraded, all of us hoping to get up there among the few.

During the time Anderson was working on the essays for *Perhaps Women,* he was strongly attracted to communism as a way out of the dilemmas of industrialism and the deepening economic depression. On every side, his fellow intellectuals were joining the party; but he mistrusted it. In 1931 he wrote to Eleanor Copenhaver, "I may conceivably go to communism." Yet he could not. A few weeks later he wrote to Edmund Wilson, "I suppose the Negroes are good Communist material; but they'll be making a mistake, won't they, if they take that material just because it is easy?" On his lecture tour that fall he pondered the movement carefully. To Theodore Dreiser, he expressed his suspicion that communism might be a more intense, deadlier puritanism than had ever existed before.

Nevertheless, he continued to visit and support strikers in the South, joining with John Dos Passos and others in publishing *Harlan Miners Speak* in 1932; this was an attempt to articulate the needs and hopes of the Harlan County, Kentucky, coal-mine strikers. During this time he was writing a new *Beyond Desire,* an honest one. It was published in 1932.

In *Beyond Desire* Anderson provides the record of the war he had predicted in *Poor White* as he saw it waged in the mill and mining towns. The novel not only draws on his observations in the South but it reflects his own uncertainties. Written in a confused time by a man who had not yet made up his mind about the proper course for his country or his people, it contains more of the genuine flavor of its age than any of Anderson's other novels. In it, the problem is neither retreated from nor rejected; it is squarely faced.

In this novel Anderson has gone beyond the story of the industrial revolution and incorporated everything he has learned about the South, its people, its traditions—the psyche that gives it its regional identity. *Beyond Desire* is an attempt at another *Winesburg, Ohio*; using four short interrelated novels rather than stories and sketches as the main focus of the book, it gives him the opportunity to range widely in his analysis of the New South. Although it is another of Anderson's stories of rejection and rebellion, it goes beyond the mystic rejection in the earlier novels and shows the evolution of the change itself.

Book One, "Youth," describes the social background of the South, as seen through the story of Red Oliver; in it, Anderson contrasts the "few" with the "many." The new Southern society exists on three levels: the members of the old families who are long-established, financially secure, and traditionally powerful in the community; the newcomers from the North who, as supervisors and engineers, are primarily concerned with getting cloth manufactured as quickly, efficiently, and economically as possible; and at the bottom, the mill workers, poor whites from the town and the hills. A middle ground between the "few" and the "many" is almost nonexistent, and the small number of Negroes in the mill town is considered to be equally nonexistent—exploited and tolerated, but ignored.

The rigid line between classes is illustrated by the fact that the town has two baseball teams—one for the town, one for the mill. They do not play each other but play their counterparts from other towns, since "For the town team to have played the mill boys would have been almost like playing niggers." Against that background, Red Oliver is faced with a decision. The son of the respected town physician and a woman considered to be poor white trash by the Negroes, he has been exposed to radical theory in the Northern college he had attended. With the death of his father, he is forced to work in the mills. Having been a high school baseball star, he is expected to play and he must now choose a team. Not quite belonging to the town group because of his mother, yet suspected by the mill workers, he chooses the mill team, made up of his mother's people, with whom he has begun to feel increasingly sympathetic.

In the background of this book, Anderson introduces the mills, the machines, the specter of advancing technology, and the girls who run the machines. Book Two, "Mill Girls," is devoted to Doris Hoffman, the strongest of the mill girls, and their natural leader. She is Anderson's portrayal of the monument in stone that he had wanted to see erected as he mused about the mill girls at the end of *Nearer the Grass Roots*. Doris is the symbolic mother; she provides the link from her earliest ancestress in *Windy McPherson's Son* to her immediate predecessor, Alice, in *Alice and The Lost Novel*. But Doris, like Alice, is no longer inarticulate; she has verbally as well as spiritually accepted total responsibility for her weaker, less wise, sister workers.

Anderson points out that the mill girl, in her insecurity and servitude to the machines, can survive only by making herself indispensable through hard work, skill, and efficiency. In one of the best passages in the book he describes Doris's attempt to find diversion and relaxation at a fair. Coming so soon after *The American County Fair*, it might be expected that there would be similarities between the two books; but the dissimilarity is almost shocking. In the former, Anderson had shown the spontaneity and depth of feeling, the age-old celebration of fertility, the closeness of the fair in spirit to the earth from which its products and celebrants had sprung. But this is a new sort of fair, one in which the machine age penetrates to every corner of consciousness with a constant assault on the senses—from the thrilling mechanical rides to the machine-produced Coca-Colas and Milky Ways that the fairgoers consume mechanically—a mechanical ovation to the industrial age.

The fair "fed Doris Hoffman's consciousness of worlds outside her own mill-bound world," but it was merely an indication that the world outside is an enlarged version of her own world, dominated by the machine, by the feverish desire to consume machine-made products, and by the specter of insecurity. "The fair was crowded and your shoes got dusty and the shows were shabby and noisy but Doris didn't know that," Anderson says; she, like so many others, knows no other life.

The fair is a fake; it is a bit of opium thrust at the mill workers, but its drugging effect soon wears off and they have nothing and they know it. The only hope they have is the union; at least, that may give them some measure of control over their own lives in the future. But organizing a union is flying in the face of the power behind the machine, and they are afraid, even though they are driven to organize by the emptiness of their lives. Nevertheless the union, as it grows, fills their emptiness with hope. "Mill Girls" provides the muted obbligato accompanying the song of revolution that Anderson is directing toward its crescendo. It is restrained; it is pointed; it provides the key to the theme of revolution.

Book Three, "Ethel," shifts the scene again to another aspect of the revolution. This book describes the efforts of a woman to escape both the restraints of Southern convention and the newer demands of materialism so that she can assume the leadership that Anderson had pleaded for in *Perhaps Women*. Ethel Long, who meets Red Oliver in the town library, is a product of the old Southern mores. Like him, she has read widely and has had the same impulses of human equality, fulfillment, and understanding. The many double standards of Southern life annoy her: the reverential attitude toward white women held by Southern men while at the same time the tan population increases; the puritanism that makes the South the Bible Belt, at the same time welcoming the exploitation of industrialism; the social stratification that makes Red Oliver hover between the two extremes of Southern white civilization. In Red, Ethel sees a symbol of hope for the South in a blending of the two extremes. But Red is unaware that she sees hope in his socially ambiguous position, and they become friends as he comes to the library more and more often; at first because he has nowhere else to go, and later because he wants to learn.

Ethel's father is an effective representation of the old South as it moves into its new status. Having inherited faith in the old ways and beliefs, he accepts the new industrial faith that is introduced to him by the clergy, the wealthy, and the established, all authorities whom he knows and respects. He is incapable of questioning either faith; he can only accept. Anderson is neither unsympathetic nor vindictive in this portrayal; he shows sympathy with the paradox of the man's position, and he regrets that the man is not only incapable of questioning but afraid to question. Here, Anderson implies, is the real tragedy of the modern South: the refusal to acknowledge that the problems exist. It is against this state of mind that Ethel Long contends.

Ethel's past has been a series of contradictions almost as complex as those of the South. She wants wealth and position, and yet she does not; she wants the same sexual freedom men have, and yet she

is afraid of its brutality and sordidness; she wants to be an intellectual, but she is suspicious of intellectual shallowness and superficiality. Her rebellion is resolved when she becomes the town librarian,
a gesture considered daring for a girl of good family. A flirtation
with a scheming, unscrupulous, ungentlemanly politician amuses and
flatters her; but she is drawn to Red Oliver, and eventually they
have a brief affair. Faced with the impossibility of going on with the
affair and afraid that nothing more will come of it, she marries the
politician. She does not dare to think beyond the marriage; yet she
sees in him the reflection of the New South.

In this section Anderson finds that his hope expressed in *Perhaps
Women* is not valid, that women are unable to assume the responsibility he was so willing to give them even when they have the desire,
the capabilities, and the willingness to do so. In rejecting Red Oliver,
whom she might have saved from destruction, Ethel has made the
outcome of Red's struggle inevitable. Her desires to be strong, to be
responsible, and to be free are too much for her, and the fears and
conflicts raised by her background are insurmountable. In despair she
casts herself into the midst of the new brutality, a move that can end
only in her destruction as an individual.

In telling Ethel's story Anderson is dealing with forces that are
more complex and more diverse than any he had dealt with previously, and the result is confusion that is probably deliberate on
Anderson's part. The evidence that he presents destroyed his theory
of the eventual control of the new age by its women, since women are
also bewildered by the array of conflicting ideologies that have destroyed the potential of men. But, as dispassionately as he can,
Anderson reports the facts as he sees them, in spite of his personal
involvement in their results. The inherent paradoxes that he sees in
the confusion of personal and social values is as confusing to Ethel
Long as it was to his adolescents, who much earlier had ventured
away from the race track into the world, and her bewilderment is as
pathetic.

Book Four, "Beyond Desire," deals with the climax of the worst
war of all as it carries Red Oliver to his inevitable end. After his rejection by Ethel, he wanders aimlessly through the South, and as
this book opens, he awakens confused, and then remembers that he
is in a strikers' camp, where he has been mistaken for an expected
Communist leader. Oliver's confusion persists, however, and he is
unable either to deny or to affirm that he is a Communist, thereby

reflecting the uncertainty that Anderson himself felt at this time. Red thinks to himself:

> "Perhaps I would like to be the thing you think I am. I don't know. Anyway I'm not.
>
> "If the thing you think I am is something fine and brave, then I would like to be it.
>
> "I want that: to be something fine and brave. There is too much ugliness in life and people. I don't want to be ugly."

If being fine and brave means to be a Communist, then Oliver is willing to be so named; but Oliver, like his creator, would have reservations to this appellation under different conditions. It is significant that the emphasis here is not on economic or political beliefs but on relationships to people and to an ideal. This is essentially the way that the strikers see communism: it promises them that they will no longer be ugly. However, Oliver is still confused, but he remembers that he had almost unconsciously told a motorist who had given him a lift that he is a Communist; later, he finds that the motorist told the police who are now searching for him. Still, he is unable to make up his mind. Actually what is happening around him is the fulfillment of Anderson's prophecy in *Beyond Desire*:

> There were new words, new ideas, striking on the consciousness of people. The words themselves bothered Red. "Communism, socialism, the bourgeoisie, capitalism, Karl Marx." The bitter, long struggle that had to come . . . the war . . . that was what it would be . . . between those who had and those who couldn't get . . . . There would be all sorts of queer new alignments of people in life . . . new alignments made, having to be made. In the end every man and every woman, even the children, would have to line themselves up on the one side or the other.

Both Anderson and his hero knew which side they were on; Anderson had made public his alignment in *Harlan Miners Speak*, and Oliver had participated in a strike at his home-town mill and had fled when it was broken. Red had seen brutality on the Communist's side; "he had got just enough of communism, its philosophy, to make him afraid. He was afraid and at the same time fascinated. He might at any moment surrender, become a communist . . . . He wanted to go. He didn't want to go." He knew that communism meant the most brutal sort of war, and yet he was afraid that there was nothing else.

This is the indecision and confusion that drew the caustic comments of some critics of the book, both at its appearance in 1932 and more recently. The earlier critics, many of whom had gone over or thought they had or said they had because it was stylish, have a position that is understandable; Anderson was to them that anachronistic political phenomenon, a mugwump. But critics with the advantage of perspective should know better. Just as the times and countless numbers of young Americans themselves were drifting, physically and intellectually to communism, so was Red Oliver— drawn and yet repelled.

This section, more than any other in the book, reflects the kaleidoscopic structure of the times, the indecisions, the search for a firm and promising hand. Its quick, vivid sketches of the workers show their backgrounds, their fears, and their hopes. Occasionally a doubt comes through, almost in anguish: " 'How do I know that I give a damn for people in general, the generality of people . . . their suffering? It may be all bunk?' " But Anderson's deep compassion as well as his often implied question answers that: " 'Oh, hell, it's true [that] those who are always getting it in the neck are the nicest people. I wonder why.' " In the end his hero, Red Oliver, gets it in the neck. In an encounter with the militia, led by a young officer who is also one of the "nicest people," Red steps forward, still uncertain of the label that should be pinned on him but certain of the side to which he is aligned, and is shot dead. The question has been resolved; names are not important, nor is political or social theory. Man's willingness to act on the side of his sympathies is the only ultimate meaning in the struggle.

Beyond Desire is not a novel about communism nor is it a call to revolution. Rather, it is a portrayal of a time, place, and combination of circumstances that gave rise to more indecision and self-interrogation than has any other time in American history except the Civil War. Anderson has attempted to cram all this atmosphere and background into his novel, giving rise to the charges of formlessness, meandering, and irrelevancies that have been leveled against it. But if the novel is formless and confused, so were the times that produced it, and Anderson, as fascinated by the events and as naturally sympathetic to those caught up in them as he was, produced a novel that, like *Poor White,* is a social document accurately reflecting the spirit of the age. Anderson the townsman, secure in his personal identity and in his place, looked out at the world, reported what he saw, and mirrored effectively the spirit of those observations; yet, canny in his role he refused to permit himself to be labeled. Instead he was willing to be counted on the side of humanity, justice, and courage.

In *Beyond Desire*, as in *Tar* and in the later *Kit Brandon*, Anderson wrote another of his almost good novels. In spite of his earlier declaration that he was through with hurried work and that he would take his time and ignore pressures, this novel suffers both structurally and stylistically from his desire to get it done and through the presses. Parts of it are handled with care, resulting in writing as good as he had ever done, especially in the portion dealing with the mill girls. This section, for its economy, grace, and intensity, is reminiscent of *Winesburg*. Elsewhere, however, he resorted to the jerky rhythms conducive to easy writing, and the novel suffers accordingly. His haste is partially understandable; he was finishing another novel—he had not written one in seven years—and he saw it as an opportunity to restore his literary reputation; but the haste was unwise.

While *Beyond Desire* was on the presses, Anderson joined the American delegation to the left wing World's Congress against War, which met in Amsterdam in August and September of 1932. Although Communist delegates were in the majority, Anderson was impressed by the seeming harmony of the meeting. He made a brief speech on the problems of the artist in America, but for the most part he remained in the background, seeing in the gathering something of the mystic unity that he had sought to portray in *Marching Men*. As in the novel, he did not look beneath the surface harmony or, in this case, read carefully enough the adopted "Manifest—War Congress against the Imperialist War" to see how effectively Communist domination had made the congress an instrument of its own ends.

However, shortly after his return from Amsterdam, his renewed faith in his creative ability led him to start a never-finished autobiographical work called *A Book of Days*, parts of which were later incorporated in the *Memoirs*; to put together a new volume of short stories, *Death in the Woods*; and to work on a stage version of *Winesburg, Ohio*. At the same time, his relationship with Eleanor Copenhaver was moving steadily toward marriage. As a result, his interest in the political and economic scene began to wane temporarily, and the end of his indecisive flirtation with the Communist party came at this point.

Having written to Tom Smith, his editor at Liveright, that he was too much concerned with the individualist's point of view to accept the dogma of the Communist party, although the philosophy of communism and of the individual might coincide at times, he told Smith that he had decided not to go over. In a later series of letters to Russian editors who had evidently wanted to exploit his interest for propaganda purposes, he made clear that he was interested in the movement but did not accept it. To the editor of the Soviet *Literary Gazette,* who had criticized his work as being overly concerned with bourgeois psychology, he pointed out that his own best contribution to human dignity was his work. At this time Anderson wrote "Brother Death," one of his best stories, for inclusion in the *Death in the Woods* collection. Then, perhaps reassured by the foreshadowing of the New Deal, he gave his attention to personal affairs, making notes for novels, traveling, and looking forward to the publication of *Death in the Woods.* This volume, he was sure, contained some of his best work.

In *Death in the Woods* Anderson collected the best of the short fiction that he had written during the preceding several years, including the title story. In this book, published in 1933, he dispensed with foreword, preface, introduction, or tone piece, preferring instead that the works themselves be interpreted through their own literary art. Perhaps he no longer felt the need for explaining himself and his works as he had for so long; at any rate, the decision was a wise one. Certain that this book would be financially successful and would enhance his reputation, he used a great deal of care in its preparation. Not only did he change the order and content of the volume after he had received the proofs, eliminating several stories that he felt were unsatisfactory, but he wrote "Brother Death" for inclusion. The latter was, he felt, ". . . one of the finest stories I've ever done, and I even dare to say one of the finest and most significant anyone has ever done. Sounds cocky, doesn't it?"

The comment was cocky; hardly in keeping with a mood of desperate uncertainty and fumbling creativity, which Irving Howe maintains was Anderson's state at this time.[1] Not only is the statement cocky, but it is not far from the truth. "Brother Death" and "Death in the Woods" are two of Anderson's best stories, ranking easily with those in the earlier collections; and the volume as a whole is evidence that in the short story form, Anderson's power in style and execution is at its best.

To give form to the book, Anderson again used a framing tech-

[1] Howe, *Sherwood Anderson,* pp. 237–239.

nique, leading off with "Death in the Woods" and concluding with "Brother Death," companion pieces in mood, theme, and setting. The first story is based on an incident presumably from Anderson's childhood, described at length in *Tar: A Midwest Childhood*. In it Anderson returns to the grotesque castoffs of society that have consistently been his people. The story is that of the life and death of an old woman who is exploited by her brutal husband, her son, and their dogs. The men have beaten her into perpetual silence, and her main function is to provide them with food. One night, as she is returning from the village, accompanied by the dogs, with meat given her by a kind butcher, she sits down to rest in a clearing in the snowy woods; a day or two later she is found naked and dead. The dogs had taken the meat, torn off her clothes, but had not touched her; the tracks in the snow indicated that the dogs had circled around her, reverting to their savage instincts.

In death she seems young and beautiful to the boy who looks on; she has been untouched by the years of beating and bullying, as though death has erased the marks of her tragic life. The boy always remembers the sight, but only in later years does he come to know that she was one whom life had forced to its lowest levels. As in Anderson's earlier stories dealing with adolescent initiation, the story transcends that initial theme and becomes a story of adult realization; of recognition that death is inevitable but not terrible, that it can be a release from and a compensation for the brutality and the lack of feeling one encounters in life.

The story has been interpreted as a symbolic presentation of the life and death of Anderson's own mother whom he had earlier pictured as silent and inarticulate, and who had presumably been sent to her early grave by hard work and selfless devotion. But the story is too harsh and brutal to be representative of the years he had recently seen in perspective as satisfying and rich. Moreover, after having rehabilitated the image of his father in his recent autobiographical writings, Anderson would hardly have returned to a portrayal of him that was as animalistic and as shadowy as the father in this story. Rather, he chose this stark, depersonalized presentation not to symbolize family relations but to commemorate the silent, welcome deaths that occur whenever man reduces his relations with his fellows to the level of the jungle.

In "The Return" Anderson counters the grimness of the preceding story with the realization that the machine age had replaced the past recalled by the protagonist. His only choice is to have the machine carry him quickly away from the fears brought on by that realization. "There She Is—She Is Taking Her Bath" is a seemingly humorous piece pointing out the inarticulateness of modern life and the resulting folly when man is afraid to penetrate surface barriers. The humor disappears as the impotent protagonist realizes that his fears will continue, that his hands will shake, and that he will spill his dessert.

"The Fight" is another story set in the present. It is an attempt to point out the senselessness and the irrationality at the heart of human rivalry, which no amount of reason can change. Only a change of heart can do this, Anderson points out, an act of love that cannot be intellectualized. "That Sophistication" carries this theme through to the Bohemian revolt of the twenties, pointing out that deliberately intellectualized rejection is futile, that it results in a meaningless, ritualized morass. Here again Anderson emphasizes that changes in human relations can come about only by something more far-reaching than merely willing the changes.

The other stories in the collection explore further aspects of the futility of intellectualized human relations. "In a Strange Town" points out the uselessness of the attempt to control the human experience through rational action. Such attempts fail, the wanderer in this story shows, because they try to analyze what cannot be analyzed. Human existence can only be understood through empathy and an honest approach to human lives and deaths as extensions of one's self. The mountaineer juror in "A Jury Case" realizes this instinctively as he learns that there is a difference between human truth and intellectualized legal truth; and the middle-aged doctor in "Another Wife" points out that true feeling transcends things that can be seen, felt, or measured. With true maturity comes wisdom in the form of the realization that appearance, the only thing on which man can focus his intellectual powers, is unimportant and that human emotions, if they are true, perceive this difference and penetrate to the essence of other lives. In "The Flood" Anderson points out that the scholar cannot define this ability of the human heart even though he has experienced it and will experience it again.

Through the stories in the collection, Anderson has woven a progressive thematic thread that stresses the inability of the human mind to determine the ultimate reality behind appearance and events. This thread begins with the apparent tragedy, which is not a tragedy at all, in "Death in the Woods" by emphasizing man's inability or frightened unwillingness to search for the meaning beneath the surface of human life. This, Anderson points out, results in man's attempts to rationalize his insecurities, knowing all the while that he could find the truth if he were not afraid. The theme reverses itself in the following stories, turning to the side that contains the key to any ultimate fulfillment of man's potential. The answer lies in the rejection of attempts to solve human problems through rational means and in the endeavor to build relationships on the fact that reality can be found only through a determined effort to enter into the lives of others. This, of course, is contingent upon an appreciation of the intrinsic worth not only of human life but also of death, which often provides the fulfillment that life has denied.

This thematic thread leads directly to "Brother Death," the last story in the collection and the one that Anderson wrote as a capstone in order to bring the theme to its logical conclusion. In "Brother Death" he completely reverses the conventional roles of appearance and reality. This story, like "Death in the Woods," deals with the realization that death can be life and that life can be death; but again, as in the first story, it is a realization that can come only with maturity. The story has two plots, each an amplification of the same theme. The first plot concerns a young girl and her younger brother who has a heart condition so serious that he may die at any time. In an effort to prolong his life, the family prevents him from playing normally. To the young girl, this is wrong, and finally her protests result in the boy's freedom to play. After a year or two he dies, quietly and peacefully in his sleep.

The second plot centers around the conflict between the father and the oldest son, each of whom has his own ideas about running the family farm. As a focal point for the conflict, Anderson uses two huge oak trees—beautiful and shady but useless—standing in the pasture. The father wants to remove them, but the son protests. Eventually the father has his way, and the son is torn between accepting the decision, thus protecting his position as heir, and leaving the farm. He remains on the farm; and in so doing, he surrenders his individuality to the will of his father. The girl realizes later that the physical death of her younger brother was more humane than the spiritual death suffered by her older brother. Thus, the conventional roles have been reversed: to die is to preserve one's freedom; to live is to relinquish it.

"Brother Death" is Anderson at his best. A microcosm of everything he had experienced in his long observation of America, it shows that he had at last recognized the basic factor that had corrupted American civilization: the inability to distinguish between substance and dross and the all-too-frequent willingness to accept the cheaper substitute rather than search for the more valuable. This concept goes far beyond his earlier dogma that the industrial age is one in which man, through his powers of self-delusion, believes that the standardized machine-made product is as satisfying as that product which has been made not only with skill, but with love, by an artisan who takes pride in his craftsmanship and achieves satisfaction in having made the product. Here Anderson points out that man's willingness to accept material values instead of spiritual values is responsible for the corruption of the American ideal and of the American life.

In "Brother Death" as in "Death in the Woods" Anderson points out that death of man's body can be his ultimate triumph over his environment, not because he will pass on to a perfect state, but because he is no longer faced with demands that he surrender his individuality. Whereas, to live in a state of compromise with the demands of society is to place one's individuality in danger, eventually surrendering it, and seeing it die. This is the real death that society ignores even while it denies the meaning of the other. This, Anderson says, is the unnecessary and tragic death, while the other should be celebrated as good.

The stories in *Death in the Woods* contain Anderson's most cogent and most perceptive comments on American civilization; they are the product of his experiences from boyhood to retirement in the Virginia hills. Coming at this time, as he was trying to find a solution to the Depression, and marking his disenchantment with communism, the collection is the representation of his belief that a reversal of American values was needed. If America was to survive as a nation, she had to look above and beyond the immediate surface of life for the beliefs that she needed so desperately and had lost.

The collection also gives further indication of Anderson's mastery of his craft. Always at his stylistic best in the shorter forms, he again reproduces the flat rhythms of the American Midwest, and constructs his stories in the old, oral tradition that for all its seeming formlessness is carefully controlled. *Death in the Woods* is his most consistently high level collection of stories if *Winesburg, Ohio* is excluded; and with *Beyond Desire,* it points out that he had learned to use the material that he gathered after he had had enough of withdrawal and had re-entered the world.

The common core of the criticism leveled at Anderson's work of this period is that it is "mindless," that he has failed to think his material through and to show its logical culmination. Such criticism is justified when directed at the earlier novels of personal rebellion, but such criticism was strangely lacking at that time. However, to direct it now against either *Beyond Desire* or *Death in the Woods* indicates a lack of critical perception. *Beyond Desire* is politically but not philosophically inconclusive, since it points out the necessity of man's allegiance to human dignity. *Death in the Woods* makes observations about the meaning of life and death that are keenly perceptive.

The contrast between *Beyond Desire* and *Death in the Woods* does, however, point out Anderson's real creative difficulty. His problem was not in conception of the works; it was in execution. Not only was he at his best in the shorter forms, but his inability to recognize his own stylistic strength is obvious. The short stories in *Death in the Woods* and "Mill Girls" in *Beyond Desire,* are in the Midwestern idioms and rhythms that he used in *Winesburg, Ohio,* but much of the novel is in the jerky experimental style that fascinated him to the detriment of his work. Perhaps this is mindlessness of a sort, but it is a confusion of techniques rather than conception, and the two kinds of shortcomings are easily distinguishable.

At this point Anderson was entering the last phase of both his life and his career. He was about to marry Eleanor Copenhaver, who was partially responsible for his renewed attention to his work and his world; and he had five more books to write, four of them concerned with his final statements on the meaning of the American experience as he had known it. Moreover, he was to find and support a movement that promised to bring dignity to the individual instead of demanding that he sacrifice individuality for security. During those last years, the farm and the Virginia hills were to provide a place where he could withdraw occasionally to carry out his final role as townsman—looking at the world and liking most of what he sees, at the same time renewing his fight against the forces that make grotesques out of men.

8

THE TOWNSMAN AND THE WORLD

T HROUGH an unfortunate series of circumstances, *Death in the Woods* did not aid either Anderson's financial status or his literary reputation. While it was in the presses, his publisher failed, and the book never really came out. By this time, however, Anderson was accustomed to bad breaks, and his only regret was, as he wrote to Gertrude Stein, that he had no copies to send his friends.

At the time Anderson paid little attention to the book's unfortunate demise because he was being discovered by the academic community and he was becoming increasingly concerned with the coming of the New Deal. Moreover, he and Eleanor Copenhaver were steadily drawing closer to marriage. Although there was a difference in their ages, they shared compelling interests and compassion for the people with whom they were both intimately concerned. Their common values provided the basis for the mutually fulfilling relationship that he had sought for so long.

It is impossible to determine entirely the influence that Eleanor had on his work during the years of their friendship, courtship, and marriage; but as Anderson pointed out in numerous letters, it was a great one. He gave credit to her for renewing his interest in the world after he had withdrawn in despair and for teaching him to know the victims of Southern industrialism. She apparently helped him to regain such faith in his creative powers that the old fears diminished. The marriage, which took place in July 1933, was happy for both of them.

Anderson's first book publication after his marriage was *No Swank*, a collection of short, impressionistic pieces that show his control over the shorter forms. A limited edition work, it is deserving of more attention than it has received. In it he pays tribute to people he had known who, without pretense or self-righteousness, tried to make the world a better place in which to live and who had enriched his life. *No Swank* is the first of Anderson's work of final affirmation: it reflects the turmoil of the early Depression years and his hope as the New Deal begins to function, and it reiterates his faith in humanity.

The sketches are not, as he points out, biographical but impressionistic. In the first of them, "Meeting Ring Lardner," he tried to reveal the essence of a man who hid behind a mask of indifference. Anderson points out the carefully concealed compassion reflected in the attitude of Lardner's friends toward the man. For a moment Anderson reveals Lardner with the mask off, a shy man reaching out for understanding. In "Death on a Winter Day" Anderson writes a tribute on the death of his friend Leon Bazalgette in which he recaptures Bazalgette's feeling for life. "The Dreiser" is a study in contrasts between the outspoken Theodore Dreiser who asserts that he is right and the shy, sensitive, uncertain man behind the façade. Like Lardner, Anderson suggests that Dreiser, too, was compelled to wear a mask. In "J. J. Lankes and his Woodcuts" Anderson acknowledges Lankes as being one of the significant artists of the day, while "Two Irishmen" recounts the hunger for life that possesses Fred O'Brien and Maurice Long.

"To George Borrow" and "Gertrude Stein" are Anderson's recognition of his debts to each of them, and "A Man's Mind" and "Lawrence Again" not only recognize his literary debt to D. H. Lawrence but emphasize Lawrence's efforts to broaden men's understanding. "Margaret Anderson: Real—Unreal" and "Paul" are tributes to old friends. The latter is Paul Rosenfeld, to whom Anderson had been close for a long time.

The three most revealing essays are "A Stonewall Jackson Man," "Lincoln Steffens Talks of Russia," and "No Swank." The first is an obituary reprinted from one of Anderson's newspapers, in which Anderson, in effect, writes the obituary of the old ways of individualism as it is destroyed by the new industrialism. The old rebel yell of individualism, Anderson notes, is heard no more, yet man's enduring spirit has not been lost.

"Lincoln Steffens Talks of Russia" gives insight into what Anderson feels should be the result of the new American revolution: it should be a revolution of the way men treat each other. In Russia, Steffens says, men feel that they are building a new society. This concept excites Anderson; he hopes this atmosphere will arise in America.

"No Swank" marks Anderson's acceptance of the principles of the

New Deal, the hopes of which he personifies in Henry Wallace, Franklin D. Roosevelt's Secretary of Agriculture. Wallace's dream is to restore dignity to the American countryside; and in this essay Anderson affirms his belief not in what Russia is trying to do but in what America, led by men like Henry Wallace, is trying to do.

Viewed in its entirety, *No Swank* contains Anderson's first strong statement of faith in the future of America, a faith that America will apply the pastoral and humanistic collectivism of small-town life to the nation as a whole. Over the Depression's aura of death, Anderson projects a strong air of hope. The countryside is still here, as are the old worthwhile values, and the essays indicate Anderson's feeling that America has the men and the spirit to achieve greatness. Out of the Depression's crisis, something new and real may emerge, he avers as he concludes, "Sometimes you have made me feel that we Americans might yet, in spite of hell and high water, be a people." Like many of his contemporaries, Anderson saw the New Deal as a spiritual revolution that would lead to a national recognition of the intrinsic worth of every individual. He believed that the people to whom he pays tribute in the volume are some of those who had done much in bringing America to this new point of view.

Too often Anderson resorts to the fragmented style that marred his work in the late twenties and early thirties, and the result lessens the impact of the deep feeling with which he approached his material. But in some of the essays, especially "No Swank," he reverts to his natural style, and the end result is powerful. In these essays it is evident that Anderson is beginning to associate his old values with the world he has rejoined, and the volume provides the basis for his final statements of affirmation. It marks his withdrawal from the active search and battle for human dignity and fulfillment that had characterized most of his life, and it indicates the path his last books will take in which he sums up the meaning of the American experience as he has known it. *No Swank* bridges the gap between his search and his conclusions.

Although Anderson had begun to have faith in America's future, he could not rest, nor could he return wholeheartedly to his role of storyteller. He attempted to work on a folk opera, "The Mississippi," with Louis Gruenberg; but as he wrote Gertrude Stein, he was more interested in what was going on in America. He wanted to serve the New Deal without pay, but his precarious financial state would not permit him. Instead he accepted a commission from Raymond Moley, braintruster and editor of *Today,* to roam America and to report his observations in articles for the magazine.

Puzzled America, published in 1935, contains the record of these observations made in the Midwest and the South during 1934. Like *Beyond Desire, Puzzled America* is the record of a confused people in a confused time. In it Anderson does not propose solutions to the dilemma of the Depression, since, as he wrote to Maxwell Perkins, he has no solutions. His prime interest is in interpreting the times and the people for the benefit of his fellow townsmen and his fellow countrymen.

However, *Puzzled America* does not reflect a puzzled and bewildered Sherwood Anderson, as Oscar Cargill asserts;[1] it does clearly reflect Anderson's insight into the relationship between the people of rural and small-town America and the world in which they live as they start the long struggle upward out of the ruin brought about by rampant materialism. The people themselves are puzzled in the early 1930s, and the book is a statement of the point of view of the people whom Anderson knew as well as anyone else in America. In this book, more than any other of Anderson's last period, the country editor is at work, interpreting the times and their people for the benefit of his fellow-townsmen and fellow Americans.

In the introduction to *Puzzled America,* Anderson summarizes his observations and conclusions, revealing his amazement that there is so little bitterness in the country. The essential ingredient of revolution is missing, he says, and in its place is a bewilderment and a sense of being deprived of long held beliefs not in American democracy itself but in the leaders it had produced. This observation, more than any other, explains the overwhelming majorities that kept returning Franklin Roosevelt to the White House:

> We are the people who passed through the World War and its aftermath. We saw the upflaring of prosperity, lived through the Harding and the Coolidge times. We got the hard-boiled boys and the wise-crackers. We got, oh, so many new millionaires. As a people we are now fed up on it all.
>
> We do not want cynicism. We want belief.
>
> Can we find it in one another, in democracy, in the leadership we are likely to get out of a democracy? . . . If the leaders we, as a democracy—and we are still a democracy, very much a democracy

[1] Cargill, *Intellectual America,* p. 685.

—if the leaders we are now throwing up into places of power do not lead along new roads, if they fail us, the failure will not be due to a lack of belief.

Here was the real power behind Franklin Roosevelt, who became the symbol of belief in the 1930s; and here, in one of Anderson's least known works, is an indication of the sureness with which he was able to analyze the people left behind by the main stream of American life. *Puzzled America* not only notes the wreckage wrought by materialism but it gives further testimony to Anderson's faith in the belief that geography and humanity go together in the composition of America.

In the first part of the book, devoted to the South, Anderson points out the need for a belief that will serve as catalyst to start again the intimate, functioning relationship between human and natural resources. In "At the Mine Mouth" he notes that in America, there is enough unused power to run half the country, but among the men, he sees a new sense of identification between citizen and government that gives promise for the future. In a brief, positive sketch Anderson makes this promise vivid in his portrayal of a Negro coal miner, who says, " 'We have been like hogs rooting in the woods for acorns. . . . We have had our eyes on the ground but now we are beginning to look up.' "

"The Price of Aristocracy" examines the archaic set of beliefs in the South that have abused both the land and the people. However, Anderson sees a new set of beliefs emerging that look to identification with the rest of the country and with a concerned and directed government in place of the distorted notions of chivalry and self-pity that had occupied the Southern consciousness for so long. The section called "People" is more effective than any other part of the book. In it Anderson turns to a series of brief, personal sketches that catch the flavor of this new search in the South for a belief to replace the old ways.

In "A Rural Realist" Anderson introduces a woman who sought the new faith, attaining dignity in the process. In "He Found His Racket," he portrays her male counterpart, a panhandler who does not mind his nomadic existence too much because he knows that "pretty soon" he'll go back to work as an electrician. The vignettes continue: an old farmer who lost his farm but wants to go back to his way of life; the eagerness and interest of a young CCC worker aiding in archeological excavations; the man who sees in TVA the beginnings of the New America. Reforestation, reclamation, and other conservation projects in the CCC camps encourage Anderson, because the ravages of insatiable greed are being rectified by a sane and worthwhile government program, and, above all, the boys themselves are being reclaimed.

Throughout his observations of the South, Anderson states again and again that the Southerners show both bewilderment and a renewed sense of hope on realizing that someone, somewhere in government cares about them. In the tobacco country, a man defines the New Deal as meaning ". . . that people have got to be made to quit cutting each other's throats"; in an unemployed millworker Anderson sees an "undying so-American optimism" that borders on the pathetic; in a Southern doctor he finds a compassion transcending that demanded by his calling; in "A Union Meeting" he observes the poor sharing with the poorer. There is hope as well as hunger in the South, he notes, as he turns toward the agricultural heart of the upper Middle West.

Here, too, he notes the greedy exploitation that had ruined much of the South. Farms were being blown away even more rapidly than they were foreclosed, as drought combined with the economic collapse to drive men from the land, and men alone were helpless to do anything about either calamity. Instead they looked to one another and to Washington for the help they needed and could not find in the myth of rugged individualism. Anderson epitomizes this new belief in an encounter with a little old tramp printer who distributes his own pamphlets setting forth the demand for a new people-oriented government. He reiterates this belief in the portrait of a people who can dance even though they are on relief.

Further indication, if any is needed by this time, of Anderson's rejection of the Communist solution is found in his description of a little corn town in the Middle West when he reaffirms both his faith and his hope in America and in a native American way, free from chaos. He states the need for a new American belief that will enable man to destroy only the evils of the old ways and to build something new that is truly American. He concludes that here in the heart of America he has found the belief that life in America can become the good life, a belief echoed everywhere he has visited—in the mining and mill towns as well as on the farms and in county seats.

In his concluding essay, "The Return of the Princess," he records the plea of a stranger to America, a refugee noblewoman, whom he had encountered at Roosevelt's inauguration in 1933. In words not his own yet completely expressive of that faith in the American ideal he always believed achievable, he quotes the woman:

> "You in America, in spite of all the desperate position you may now be in, may be again what you were. You were once the hope of the world, the place to which the oppressed came. You may be it again . . . . There must be one strong land in the world to which no dictator comes, to which the creeping fear does not come."

Puzzled America is a cross section of America in the midst of the most severe economic upheaval it has ever experienced. Like *Beyond Desire* it is a valuable social document as it reaches out to the people of the rural and industrial areas in the attempt to help them understand both their predicament and themselves. In its own right the book testifies to the people's faith in their own ability to lift the country out of economic chaos. Just as they had made a wilderness into a productive homeland a generation or two before and had attained dignity in the process, they believed that they were going to construct a new, responsible society that accurately reflected the needs, hopes, and dreams of the people. This is far from a cry for upheaval and revolution, either by Anderson or by the grass roots spokesmen, but it is a hope and a plea for the destruction of the perverted concepts of individualism that had resulted in exploitation and collapse. The means by which the people could bring about this destruction was the democratic process; they would put men into power who would act and who would return dignity and self-respect to those who had been deprived of it.

The results of Anderson's accurate and unappreciated analyses of the people of the times have become history. The people selected a man who could act, and the results of his actions have changed America into a country that would be unrecognized by the propagators of the gospel of wealth. The Wagner Act, TVA, Social Security, and other acts of social legislation were the result of the fusion of democratic strength, American faith, and the leadership of a man who could transmute dreams into actions. The combination gave Sherwood Anderson's people much of the dignity and self-respect that he sought for them.

Puzzled America, like *Hello Towns!* is ostensibly journalism, but Anderson had shown in the earlier book that it was not necessary to stop with mere rote recitation of fact. Here he applies the same approach to a much larger scene. The result is a collection of sketches of the people as he found them to be: representative of the spirit of America in a way that borders on a new kind of folklore, a folklore of faith and humility instead of bluster and pride. In doing so, Anderson points out that there are not many Americas—rural America, industrial America, southern America, midwestern America, and others—but only one America—the America he depicts in this volume. Therefore, Anderson synthesizes apparent diversity with underlying basic unity to make clear the theme of the book: a people's search for faith.

Although *Puzzled America* was a financial failure, it contains some of Anderson's best writings and it is worthy of much wider attention than it has received. In this volume, as in *Hello Towns!,* Anderson attempts to transcend the immediate and to show the universal implications of his subject matter. In doing so he has returned to the old *Winesburg* style, combining it with his intuitive approach to understanding the people; and he has been largely successful. Unfortunately its subject—the Depression—limits its appeal in spite of the fact that the book shows what journalism can be.

Puzzled America is not a prophetic book in the sense that Anderson foresaw the specifics of the social revolution of the 1930s—although he gave voice to the demand for that change. Over and over again, with a faith reminiscent of Herbert Hoover's belief that America was fundamentally sound, Anderson restates his belief that America itself is all right. But Hoover and Anderson were talking about two different America. Hoover's faith was in the economic structure that had rewarded him liberally and had engendered his faith in the old concepts of paternalism; Anderson's faith was in the land and in the people and in their ability to cooperate in producing a richer, more meaningful world through the democratic process. Anderson's America was one that had been forgotten by the Hoovers.

In effect *Puzzled America* marks another of Anderson's rejections, this time, of any alien political or economic system, including communism. After his return to the security and meaningfulness of the American past that he rediscovered in the hill country of Virginia, he had been drawn back into combat against the rampant forces of materialism. But he recognizes that Marx had no panacea. America's only hope, he feels, lies in the values that had drawn him to Virginia.

During the remaining six years of his life, Anderson lived much more quietly than he ever had. Happily married and feeling secure, he spent most of his time at Ripshin Farm, leaving it only for winter trips farther south and to Mexico, and for visits to old friends. After *Puzzled America* had been completed, he worked with Jasper Deeter of the Hedgerow Theatre, an experimental group in Pennsylvania, on a dramatic version of *Winesburg, Ohio,* which, when Deeter produced it, was successful. However, Broadway was not interested. The production was a good adaptation, but the power that marked the original version could not be transferred successfully to another medium, and the dramatic version is inferior to the book.

Meanwhile Anderson's mind was full of other creative projects, most of them dramatic adaptations, from *Dark Laughter,* from *Marching Men* (of which he wrote to Roger Sergel that he was fascinated by the effects that might be had by experimentation with sound), and in a play thematically close to *Poor White,* which he had tentatively entitled *They Shall Be Free.* He also turned to the Civil War and Lincoln. In his preoccupation with the American ability to rise above crisis, he read everything on both subjects that he could find, planning eventually to use the material in a study he hoped would epitomize the American story. Of this unrealized dream, a fragment exists, possibly written as early as 1924 and unpublished until Paul Rosenfeld's *Sherwood Anderson Reader* appeared in 1947. It is unfortunate that this project, which was based on a life that he saw as the essence of American life, was never finished. Perhaps he could not finish it because in his own mind he was too closely identified with America's recurring crisis.

In the summer of 1935 he began sustained work on his last novel, *Kit Brandon,* an effort that he found tiring. Published in 1935, *Kit Brandon* is a combination of solid Anderson writing and of hurried, almost frenzied prose that seems to indicate his desire to finish it, put it on paper and be done with it. Growing out of his continued interest in the Southern mountain girl, and based on his observations of the widespread bootlegging industry in the Virginia hills, it is an attempt to fuse the two into a novel that would provide for all time his monument to the mountain girl and her embodiment of the realistic environment from which she came. He almost succeeded, and there are many indications that had he given as much attention to this novel as he had to the earlier ones, he would have written his best novel. Although it ranks below the artistic level of his collections of shorter works, in many ways it remains close to his best efforts.

Anderson's approach to *Kit Brandon* is a technique that he had never used before: he is a sympathetic listener to whom Kit tells her story. Partially as a result of his previous fiction role of observer-interpreter-storyteller and partially as a result of a carefully controlled objectivity, the novel is the best constructed of any of Anderson's long works. The subject matter allows him to feel deeply sympathetic with the people and yet, as with the miners and weavers he wrote about in *Puzzled America,* remain sufficiently detached so that he can see them as human beings rather than as extensions of himself or as objects of pity. The result is Anderson's only major fictional attempt to analyze the strength and individualism of the Southern hill people among whom he lived.

Kit is a mountain girl, a product of the sort of brutal innocence that Anderson had been concerned with since *Winesburg* and that he had rediscovered in the Southern hills. Her family, like so many of the others in the hills, finds it more convenient and more profitable to measure its corn in gallons rather than bushels. Her father is a man who, given the opportunity, can go far; her mother is a nonentity. At 15 Kit bears all the responsibility for the home— such as it is, also serving as lookout while the moonshine is cooking; and at 16, like so many of the other hill girls, she runs off to get a job in the mills.

After several years in the mills, during which her reading has been guided by a sympathetic woman whom she had met in a library, she gets a job in a store where she meets and eventually marries Gordon Halsey, the weak son of a wealthy and highly successful bootlegger. Kit provides Gordon with the strength he lacks, but after their marriage the relationship deteriorates. Kit leaves him and, at first for the thrill but later primarily for the material returns, she becomes a highly successful runner and decoy for the bootleg gang's operations. As she becomes increasingly notorious, she loses her desire for adventure and money. Eventually she finds that such a life is not worthwhile. When she meets a crippled young war veteran who had helped her elude the police, she wants to love and help him in return, but she knows that more than a casual relationship is impossible. Leaving him, she slips off into the night. She has learned that there are more important things in life than money and adventure, and she hopes that somewhere, somehow she may find another young man who needs her help.

This outline of the plot gives the impression that Anderson was striving for hard-boiled sensationalism typical of many novels of the 1930s, but he was not. The novel is not concerned with events, sensational or otherwise; it is concerned with the people and the land in the South, both of which Anderson had by now assimilated as thoroughly as he had his native Ohio. In the process he had learned that rural Ohio and rural Virginia were for all practical purposes identical.

In spite of the differences in style and technique, *Kit Brandon* in many respects parallels *Poor White* in theme. *Poor White* is the record of the growth of materialism around a naive and innocent Hugh McVey, who remains untouched by it until he is almost submerged in it; *Kit Brandon* deals with a girl who, like Hugh, maintains her innocence until she, too, recognizes that the material things and the adventure she seeks are meaningless. The theme with which Anderson is dealing is an old one, both in his work and in life. Three times Anderson faced evil and knew it for what it was: in business and in the modern liberation movement, both of which involved him intimately, and finally as an observer of the chaos and suffering resulting from rampant individualism and materialism. The first two produced the earlier, semiautobiographical novels, while the third, carefully controlled by Anderson's consciousness of his new role, resulted in *Kit Brandon*. In this sense it is as much the biography of an era as was *Poor White*.

Into the novel Anderson poured the knowledge of rural America that he had gained from almost a half century of wandering and feeling the pulse of the whole mid-section of the continent; and he utilized the ten years of learning to understand the relationship between his times and the people who lived in it. In combining these elements he made the novel his mature statement of the meaning of that relationship.

The first significant factor Anderson establishes in the novel is the sense of place, a reproduction of environment that is firmer and surer than anything he had previously done. Here he portrays the origin of the two-headed monster of individualism and materialism that dominated America. In the hard, uncertain life of primitive America, there was only one way that a man or woman could rise:

by the strength of his two hands and by the cunning of his mind. In such a life success could be measured only by the things accumulated in the process. Anderson had obtained the evidence for this deduction long ago, as early as the writing of *Windy McPherson's Son,* but in *Kit Brandon* he concludes for the first time that American materialism is the logical result of the circumstances under which the country was built. In this novel he portrays for the first time the cause and effect sequence, showing the strengths that might have resulted in a different, a kinder, a more understanding America if its original impetus had been less brutal and less concerned with the physical things that had to be done.

Anderson writes of the growth of modern American brutality without regret or indignation, as he would have done earlier, but in his description of its origins there is a new note of acceptance. Just as the protagonists in the earlier novels had not understood or accepted the nature of America, neither does Kit Brandon in this novel. However, Kit realizes that she must struggle against a cultural accumulation of more than 200 years through an intuitive awareness like that sensed by Sam McPherson, Hugh McVey, and the others. She believes that there are values to be found in human relationships rather than in things, but she, like the others, can only grope for them.

Full understanding of the cultural phenomena that led to Kit's predicament is left to Anderson, who, as an interested and sympathetic bystander, can only hope that someday she will rise above it and come to an intuitive but precise appreciation of human worth. Here is the real meaning of Anderson's comment in *Puzzled America* that there is enough unused power locked up in the hills to run the country. It is the human power, now confused and misdirected, that will eventually rise out of materialism to bring about a society devoted to seeking and eventually finding understanding and love.

Anderson has gone beyond the recognition of the origins of American materialism, however, and has made especially clear the relationship between man and his mechanical environment. He shows the sterility in modern life that makes such a relationship necessary. Human intercourse, he points out, was impossible, not only for Kit but for almost all the people whom she met. The barriers to communication between men are made up of things. In a competitive situation in which not enough material things are available or released for general consumption, the result can be and often is jungle

warfare or fratricide unless man learns to combine his own interests
with those of others for the common good. This unity is what
Anderson had earlier hoped would result from the union movement,
a movement with which Kit was in sympathy. Yet, with her shrewd
and skeptical insight into the savage side of human nature, Kit was
highly suspicious of such movements.

Kit's skepticism about human nature resulted in a spiritual barrier
between her and others. In the novel Anderson symbolizes this barrier both by her apparent sterility throughout her marriage and
numerous affairs, and by her willingness to use sex as a bargaining
point in the struggle for things. These factors result in her isolation
from others and Kit finds a measure of fulfillment only while she is
driving the high powered cars as a rumrunner. For most of the
novel, the cars become extensions of her own drive; in subordinating
and adapting herself to them she finds a sense of identity and
purpose impossible in her relationship with other human beings.

This relationship between Kit and the automobile is not compensation for her inability to assume the male sexual role as Freudian-
oriented critics have maintained. Rather, Anderson suggests, it is
symptomatic of a culture in which machines dominate and puritanism prevails. Such a culture prohibits meaningful relationships
among men and offers in substitution a sense of power through
service to the machine. Just as he had earlier noted the emasculation
of the men by the machines in the textile mills, he now fears that
the women may lose their femininity through a false sense of freedom, and suffer a similar fate.

The time Anderson selected for the novel is another indication
that he had grasped the meaning of the American experience in his
time. At the Coolidge-Hoover peak of materialistic prosperity, Kit
is the epitome of the adman's gospel of material accumulation and
consumption. But her acceptance of this faith is intensified into an
antisocial, antilegal nightmare. The admen proclaim that things
should be procured and consumed, and Kit is merely pursuing the
material ideal as quickly and as efficiently as the admen demand.

The prohibition setting is equally important. Prohibition was the
last direct effort of a puritan minority to impose its will on the
majority by legislation. The ensuing "noble experiment" was designed to appeal to both the idealistic and the practical. To the
former it was an opportunity to usher in a clearheaded era free
from poverty and crime; to the latter it was an opportunity to rid

the nation of an influence that detracted from the pursuit of its proper business. Both claims were nonsense to Anderson; consequently in the novel he points out the irony implicit in the prohibition amendment. Those who profited most by it and who were accumulating the things by which society measures human worth were also undermining the legal and moral codes of the society that made their existence possible. Through the resulting lawlessness, not only the system itself but the lives and property of its supporters were in jeopardy. Both materialism and puritanism, he points out, carry within themselves the seeds of their own destruction.

In the passage describing a tubercular young millworker's ability to imitate a horse or a bear while he is walking on all fours, Anderson is at his interpretive best. In this section he expresses the eagerness of man to break through flesh and convention to make himself both more and less than he is by emulating animals, which have the integrity and beauty denied to man. Here, as graphically as in "Hands," Anderson symbolizes man's impotence and frustration when he tries to communicate his own desires and needs to his fellows. Kit is entranced by the young man's antics. She understands what he expresses but she does not know why, and she is unable to articulate her understanding.

In concept, in execution, and in scope, *Kit Brandon* is as complex as any of Anderson's other novels and more evocative of subtleties. It represents Anderson's final appraisal of the meaning of American civilization, its origins, and its ultimate destiny, typifying the whole of America in a small, seemingly isolated segment. The novel might have been one of the best of its time had it not been marred by mechanical and structural difficulties; grammatical lapses and transitional disruptions are annoying, especially because they could have been easily eliminated. Unfortunately, when the proofs arrived at Ripshin Farm, Anderson disregarded them as though he was through with the novel forever; the proofs were returned uncorrected, and the flaws remain to detract from the effectiveness of what might have been his best novel.

Even while he was writing it, Anderson seems to have been aware that *Kit Brandon* would be his last attempt to write a major novel. In spite of his continued interest in the Civil War, he dropped his plans to write his interpretation of it, and although he was disappointed at the reception and sales of *Kit Brandon*, he really was not concerned. Rather, his last four years were probably the happiest

of his life. His ideological battles had been fought and won, as he
pointed out in a letter written, but never sent, to Paul Rosenfeld,
his marriage to Eleanor Copenhaver was both happy and stimulat-
ing; and his family was nearby—Robert running the papers, John
assisting him and painting, and his daughter Marion and her husband running a country paper in North Carolina. Ripshin Farm
became the refuge and base he had originally intended for it, and
his excursions were only interludes away from what had become his
home.

Anderson maintained his interest and participation in political,
economic, and especially artistic affairs during these last years.
He worked on what he called "Rudolph's Book of Days," a work
that eventually became the *Memoirs*; he continued his interest in
the theater; and he devoted much attention to the Spanish Civil
War, lending his name to numerous anti-Fascist and antitotalitarian
organizations. "It is," he wrote at this time, "the one thing I would
go to any lengths for, to defeat dictatorship, either Communist or
Fascist." Preparing his plays for publication occupied some of his
attention in 1937, and his interests in the machine age continued.
If his attitude seems vacillating and undirected during this time, a
letter to Roger Sergel goes far to explain the attitude of a man of
60 at the end of a long creative career:

> I got the copy of the magazine put out by the University of Chicago
> students . . . but as for writing something that they might want, I
> am a little doubtful.
>
> The trouble is, Roger, that I am no longer young. I certainly sym-
> pathize with and admire the enthusiasm and determination of Chris
> and his friends, but as to just where they are going, or where any of
> us is going, I have these dreadful times of doubt. As you get older,
> and perhaps a bit more sophisticated, you are eternally asking your-
> self questions that can not be answered. The truth is that we are
> probably all headed for something, but whether it will be better or
> worse than what we have I don't know . . . .
>
> The great difficulty with me in all this matter of going somewhere
> is that I am not terribly interested in arriving. My chief interest is
> what happens on the way, and this makes me a bum revolutionist.

The truth is that Anderson was tired, that he felt he was finished
with his work of recording what had happened on the way, and that
he was happy and secure in his personal life. During these years
his attention was devoted increasingly to the place and purpose of

the artist in society, an old interest, rather than to the creative act itself. Writing and revising had taken such a toll of nervous as well as physical energy during the writing of *Kit Brandon* that he was reluctant to go through the experience again for any sustained length of time. The other interests absorbed the same sort of drive and attention that Anderson had devoted to his writing, and he remained happy. However, the difficulties that he was having with critics and finances annoyed him on the occasions that he permitted himself to think about either. Somewhat testily and yet with characteristic honesty, he expressed his views on these matters to Paul Cullen in late 1937:

> I think I should write you at once to get something straightened out. It is about my getting it in the neck. You are all wrong there . . . . It's true that among American writers who have got a lot of attention I've probably made less money than any of them. Well, what of it? I haven't found that the ones who have made a lot of dough have got much fun out of it.
>
> You see . . . I have had and am having a damn good life. In some way I have managed to sleep pretty well, have loved some damn fine women, wear good enough clothes, have always had a roof over my head.
>
> People . . . come along and do swell things for me. In my wanderings I've probably covered more of the country than most men. I have known, pretty intimately, practically all the outstanding men in the arts in my time.
>
> It has been a damned good life for me. It is right now. I might very well have got it in the neck a hundred times worse by being a big popular success. People do pretty nasty things to successful men. Don't go wrong on that . . . .
>
> I just wanted to get this clear with you . . . .

Returning sporadically to creative work, Anderson started a novel called *How Green the Grass* in 1937, and then another, *Brother Carl*. Later, in 1938, he started *A Late Spring*, recast it and retitled it *Men and Their Women*, and then abandoned it, all within a few months. Still later he worked intermittently on *Memoirs* and on the essay that became *Home Town*. Because of his interest in young writers, he appeared at the Writers' Conference at the University of Colorado, at Olivet College in Michigan, and at Antioch College in Ohio.

At Olivet his principal contribution was a lecture entitled *A Writer's Conception of Realism*, in which he spoke more of himself and his philosophy of life than he did of writing. Here, almost at the end of his active writing career and of his life, he reiterates certain beliefs about himself: "It must be that I am an uncurable small town man"; about the state of the world: "The old human interest of one man in another seems to have got lost somewhere"; and about writing: "The life of reality is confused, disorderly, almost always without apparent purpose, whereas in the artist's imaginative life there is purpose . . . to give . . . form—to make it true and real to the theme, not to life." As in "A Note on Realism," published in the *Notebook,* Anderson denies that his work is an attempt to reproduce life in a small town or anywhere else. It has been, he says, an attempt to understand and interpret life wherever it may be found.

His letters during these years are full of advice to young and aspiring writers. Above all, he tells them to be honest, both to themselves and to their work, and the rest will take care of itself. Anderson had at last entered into the role that he had long sought and now fully enjoyed. Secure in his place and in his own emotions he found less and less inclination to explain and to interpret, and more and more to advise; he had at last become the small-town philosopher-sage who had fought his battles and was now able to help his successors in theirs.

9

ANDERSON'S FINAL STATEMENT

D URING the last two years of his life, Anderson reached a state of personal satisfaction and equilibrium that would have seemed impossible to him ten years before; but much of his literary reputation had vanished. Nevertheless, in 1937 he was elected to the Department of Literature of the National Institute of Arts and Letters. At first he was indignant; he felt that it was one of the phoney honors that distracted men from their work. Then, the irony began to amuse him, and he wrote that he could not accept the invitation to the dinner because he had diarrhea. There is no record of the committee's response. At the same time the rise of Hitler Germany depressed him, not only because he, a pacifist, was being forced to accept the idea of a necessary war, but because he saw that the increased attention given international affairs by the Roosevelt Administration meant that the revolution in human values engendered by the New Deal would have to be delayed until Nazism and Fascism were defeated.

Nevertheless during these years he worked on his last two long works, *Home Town* and *Memoirs*. The latter was unfinished at his death. As Hitler moved into Austria, Czechoslovakia, and then Poland, Anderson, in his room lined with pictures evocative of a past that was now history, wrote these two works as a final statement of what he saw to be the meaning of the American experience. *Home Town* and *Memoirs*, together with *Puzzled America* and *Kit Brandon*, are Anderson's definitive commentary on the permanent values he had found in his life, his relationships with others, and his country.

Home Town, the last full work Anderson saw completed and published, appeared in 1940 in a shorter version as one of "The Face of America" series. Actually a long essay, illustrated by excellent photographs, the books shows that Anderson's work had come full circle and that he had returned to the literary point of departure he left

behind when he saw Bidwell, Ohio, grow into an industrial city. The
longer version was published in 1947 as "The American Small Town"
in the *Sherwood Anderson Reader.*

In both versions Anderson pays his final tribute to the town as
the solid foundation of values on which America can build a new
and human civilization rather than a material one. In his preface
Anderson indicates that the basis of this belief lies in his feeling for
the small town that had become his home: "Perhaps I am in love
with my own town of Marion and my Virginia countryside." It is a
love rooted in the human relations for which he had been seeking.

The essay is both an evocation from his readers of an understanding of a life that is close to the springs of fertility in nature and at
the same time a delineation of the meaning of that life. The small
town, he says, is America in its essence, lying as it does ". . . half-
way between the cities whence we get the ideas and the soil whence
we get the strength." Hence, to live there is to live at the center of
American life. The changing seasons are the natural mainsprings that
actuate life in the small towns, sending their impulses through the
towns and into the most complex reaches of American civilization.
At the same time the intellectual impulses reach downward out of
the complexities until they are humanized and made part of American life in the towns, where Anderson feels he is closest to the heart
of human life.

The essay uses as its framework the seasonal cycle of a year, trac-
ing through the seasons the human activities typical of each; not
only are these the chores of life, but they are the individual reactions
known only to those aware of the intimacies of the small town. Spring
is an awakening both for the land and for the people. Summer is a
time of growth and of restlessness, culminating in the days of hard
work, harvest, and fulfillment; but there are days of enjoyment,
recreation, and wandering as well. As the days shorten and fall comes,
the small town experiences gentle nostalgia as well as stark fear—
nostalgia for the fortunate, but fear for the poor, fear for survival
through the winter.

The essay does more than recount the seasons, however; it is almost a kaleidoscope of the intimate observations and knowledge possible only in the small town. All the village characters are here: the
tough, the chicken thief, the gossip, the politician, the boy who
doesn't quite have nerve enough to go into the small house on the
back street, the moralist, the merchant. The churches, the schools,

the main street, and the newspapers are shown in their proper roles; and over all is shown the influx of new ideas, humanized to fit the town situation. The essay is an elegy for a time and place that Anderson knows no longer exists and yet that he knows is part of his life. In the background the undertones of breakup are heard; the economic upheaval that started in the cities is making its way into the towns, although it is still far off.

Throughout the book there is an undercurrent of permanence and inevitability. As the seasons change from hope to fulfillment to need and then through the cycle again, Anderson emphasizes the permanence of the values that he has found in small-town life. He makes clear his belief that no matter what the physical setting may be, man will still search for and eventually find the basic value: an intimacy between men and between man and nature that teaches the meaning of life. In the small towns Anderson finds that one is his brother's keeper, and in this concept he sees the ultimate salvation of man.

In the essay Anderson returns to the *Winesburg* prose style at its best. His writing is rhythmic, it is smooth, and in the interspersed portraits of small-town life it is "real" in the sense that he used the word in his talk at Olivet. Touchingly but not sentimentally he portrays the America he had been seeking since he first turned his back on Clyde, Ohio. This is the America he had rediscovered in Marion, Virginia, as one of the last refuges of the old life and at the same time one of the preservers of the ultimate American values that he hopes to see extended after America has been purged of materialism and has returned to an age of belief. *Home Town* is Anderson's last work published in his lifetime; it symbolizes what he had learned in Clyde, Ohio, and in the years of his retreat into the hills and in roaming Depression-ridden America; and it remains his testament to what he has rediscovered to be the ultimate source of meaning and values in America.

With the publication of *Home Town* Anderson's active literary life was at an end. He worked on the *Memoirs* and on several magazine pieces, and he spent most of his time at the farm and in Marion, writing to friends and visiting with them. For the first time he had no plans for creative work, but was content to take it easy, a happy man and undoubtedly a tired man, as he had been both through most of the Virginia years. He had found the faith and the meaning of America and its institutions and people. In one of the last letters he wrote he reiterated this faith:

I have lived long enough, traveled widely enough, and have known the so-called common people enough in the United States to believe that there is, at bottom, a great store of common sense and of belief in democracy in our American people . . . As for our own democracy, why I dare say it will always be a somewhat blundering thing, but it can always cure itself.

It is easy to pick out from his letters and diaries of these last years fragments indicating dissatisfaction, frustration, and growing fears, much of which stemmed from difficulties with writing; it is even easier to accept the explanation that Anderson had finally come to realize he could no longer write. However, such an interpretation is not the truth, as *Home Town* shows. Anderson could still write; *Home Town* is a carefully written imaginative work as well as a clear statement of the values that he recognized; and it indicates that the periods of crisis he underwent during the last years were no more significant than his earlier crises.

Rather, Anderson had at this time come to the end of his evaluation of the American scene, and at the beginning of 1941 he was casting about for a new direction for his work. On February 28, 1941, with a semiofficial State Department commission and a *Reader's Digest* contract for the preparation of several articles, he turned toward South America in the search for new experiences. On March 8, he was dead. He died at Colón in the Panama Canal Zone, the victim of peritonitis. He had found the ultimate meaning of his America, and he had no place to go except back to the hillside overlooking Marion on which he is buried.

The irony of the obituary appearing in the Elyria *Chronicle-Telegram* becomes tragic by the combination of circumstances in which the appearance of *Memoirs* passed almost unnoticed. In December 1941, America went to war; in March 1942, *Memoirs* appeared, and to a nation listening to the reports of defeats in the Philippines, the book was simply not important. Critical attention was scant, reviewers commented superficially that it was the same old material, providing further evidence that Anderson had lost his creative power, and then it was ignored. None thought to evaluate it either as literature or as a definitive statement of the meaning of the American experience by a man who had devoted much of his life to defining that experience in terms of what it meant to the people who lived it.

Like Anderson's earlier autobiographical works, *Memoirs* defies classification. Not only are dates and places hazy or at times wrong, but Anderson interprets situations to suit himself, emphasizing apparent trivialities while ignoring facts that an objective biographer would consider important. In *Memoirs,* as in his other autobiographical works, Anderson was determined to create and interpret rather than record. He was concerned not with his own life but with American life, although the only source through which he could approach it intimately was through his own experience. In the preface he makes this clear:

> Is there even such a thing as a life of one's own? Is it not some illusion, some limitation in ourselves that makes us feel there is? It seems to me that all lives merge . . . . I want to use my own life as a kind of springboard . . . . I want to make my book, my rambling house of a book, a book of people . . . . There is still another desire. I would like to write a book of the mind and of the imagination. Facts elude me. I cannot remember dates. When I deal in facts, at once I begin to lie. I can't help it. I am by nature a story teller.

With this warning from Anderson it is not only possible but necessary to approach the book as imaginative literature rather than as autobiography.

James Schevill compares Anderson's approach and purpose to that of Henry Adams in his *Education,*[1] and the point is supportable. However, Anderson was not merely recounting the growth of his imagination, as Schevill comments; rather he was using the record of that growth as a springboard from which he could leap into the American experience as he had known it. He wanted to define it, and point out its meaning, its values, and its strengths at the same time that he points out its confusions and failures.

Anderson has, of course, used much of the same old material, as critics have duly noted, and his recounting of the early years is closely related in spirit to the portrayal in *Tar.* Here, however, he is not attempting to show the events through the eyes of a child; instead, he is a man aware that he is at the end of life, looking back in the attempt to portray the microcosm of American life. Looking back as an adult he sees life in the last quarter of the nineteenth century characterized by the human intimacy to which he had paid tribute in *Home Town.* It was an age in which lives merged, so that individualism was subservient to sympathy, kindness, and love. This was the America that he saw destroyed by materialism as it isolated

[1] Schevill, *Sherwood Anderson,* pp. 342–343.

and cheapened the individual by deluding him into accepting things as the ultimate value. In recounting his early advertising and commercial experience he epitomizes this substitution of values, not merely as it had deluded him, but also as it had captured the mind of America. He states that he rediscovered, during the Elyria years, that human rather than material values are meaningful, and the rest of the volume is devoted to his efforts to identify and understand those values and to rediscover them in American life. Behind this personal struggle Anderson sees an America going through the same crisis, slowly becoming aware of failure as the Depression makes clear the transience of things and the endurance of the human spirit. At the end he has returned to a life in which he can accept those permanent values and live by them, and he feels that America will do the same.

The sequence of *Memoirs* follows the cycle of American Midwestern life through the period that saw it change from an agricultural to an industrial society. But *Memoirs* is not a factual, documented history; instead it is the record of the influence of events on human life and it focuses not on the events but on the lives themselves—Anderson's own and those of the people he had come to understand and love during those years. *Memoirs* is a book about people rather than things or events, and its subject is the nature of life rather than its surface. Its theme is the understanding of the American experience, the identification of what is worthwhile in it, and the attempt to reconcile the two in life.

Out of this theme grows Anderson's final commentary on American life, stated in the curious blend of optimism and despair characteristic of his work and his life almost from the beginning. The nature of life, he points out, is tragic; man is destined to live and die alone, isolated from his fellows, unable to know or be known by them. However, the tragedy of life is unimportant to man, because by refusing to despair he finds life's meaning in spite of recognizing its tragedy; and he finds that meaning by continually trying to break down the barriers between men and by refusing to accept the inevitable. In the process men come closer to understanding and fulfillment. Meaning is not found in the end but in the means, he concludes, summing up in one phrase what he has learned: "Life, not death, is the great adventure."

In concept as well as in execution, *Memoirs* is closely related to

Winesburg, Ohio. Like *Winesburg,* it is a story of people set in a particular period in time and space and unified thematically as well as structurally through the presence of a central character. George Willard is the catalyst that makes life and experience clear in *Winesburg,* and Anderson serves the same purpose in *Memoirs.* The grotesques who people the world become human beings again just as had those of the village; although they are still isolated and alone because of the force of circumstance, nevertheless, as they are revealed they become knowable and lovable. *Winesburg, Ohio* is the story of a young man who becomes aware of the intrinsic worth of human life; *Memoirs* is the story of that young man, grown old, looking back over a life devoted to helping men know one another.

The youthful confidence that sees the possibility of removing the barriers through the easy means of love is gone. As George Willard went off into the world he saw a long life ahead in which understanding would come. Here, however, is the statement of the mature man who knows that the faith of youth is unjustified, that easy understanding will never come, and who has accepted that inherent disillusionment. In spite of this acceptance, however, he has maintained his faith in the intrinsic worth of the individual, and he still accepts the validity of searching for understanding and love and eventually coming closer to both.

Like *Winesburg, Memoirs* deals with the distinction between appearance and reality. Just as in *Winesburg* Anderson shows the increasing realization that the two are not synonymous, here, too, Anderson makes the point clear, but there is a difference. The earlier book deals with the awareness of the difference. Here Anderson describes the efforts needed to learn to distinguish between the two and to find the underlying reality. The difference betwen the two points of view is the difference between youth and age.

The structure and style of the two books are also closely related. Like *Winesburg, Memoirs* is a unified collection of sketches that are ampifications of theme rather than plotted and individualized stories or descriptive narratives. Just as each story in *Winesburg* was an attempt to remove the barrier of appearance and to make clear the essence of a human spirit at a particular moment in time, the sketches in the *Memoirs* attempt to do the same thing. Anderson is trying to show the reality underlying appearance as he has come to know it, and each sketch brings the reader closer to understanding his view of the basic dichotomy between the surface meaning of life and the real meaning of life. Thus, the individual sketches become unified by approach as well as by theme and the presence of a central figure.

In style Anderson has gone back to the natural Midwestern rhythms of *Winesburg,* abandoning the experimental style that had marred so much of his work between 1925 and 1935. As *Puzzled America, Kit Brandon,* and *Home Town* also show, he had come to realize the ineffectiveness of much of his experimentation in style and had moved back into the idioms and rhythms that were most effective, most natural, and most individual. He rejects innovation, and his style is that of the American townsman who looks at his life and world and describes them clearly and easily.

As published, *Memoirs* indicates that stylistically, structurally, and thematically it was to be a carefully controlled and planned work. Unfortunately at Anderson's death it was incomplete, existing only in manuscript pages, and the published version is the result of editing by a group of friends headed by Paul Rosenfeld. Making a book out of another man's manuscript is difficult at best, and the incomplete state of this one made the job even more difficult. Although Anderson had left an outline of the book, some of the essays remained unwritten, and in the effort to fill out the framework the editors resurrected fragments that he had written and cast aside as early as 1920. The inclusion of this material mars the finished work, detracting from its unity and effectiveness even though some sections have been developed. It is unfortunate that Anderson did not live to complete it.

Memoirs is a book that is both important and good. It is important because it provides tangible evidence that Anderson had finally reconciled experience and ideal and had come to the conclusion that although the evidence of experience indicates that life is essentially tragic, nevertheless there is meaning in life if one seeks it: the values inherent in a job well done, in an appreciative and understanding relationship with others, and in the realization that life itself was "the great adventure." It is a good book in spite of the shortcomings of the editorial work, because as conceived and partially executed, it says something worth saying about the American experience and it says it well.

During his last few years, Anderson had come a long way, and he had incorporated into his life and his work the ideal meaning for which he had searched. After his discoveries of his own identity and of a permanent place in a changing and materialistic society, he was able to identify the permanent values that continued to exist in America in spite of the powerful but misleading veneer of materialism that, he believed, had disguised the real America for so long.

This last period saw, as a result of his reaffirmation of human values, another rediscovery as important to Anderson as the earlier two. This was his rediscovery of faith in the democratic process. After examining the glib, easy solution to the problems of industrialization, materialism, and dehumanization that communism provided, he recognized that the cure was as dangerous as the malady, and he renewed his belief in the admittedly imperfect, often blundering, but nevertheless real and decisive reflection of the people's hopes and desires through American democratic procedures. That this was not an idle dream or irrational hope he saw demonstrated as the New Deal effected the revolution in the relationship between government and the individual that he had sought; and he saw, too, that the Americans he loved gained stature and dignity as a result. In response to the democratic will rather than to an alien ideology, the focus of government shifted from a philosophy that encouraged the tyranny of materialism to one that provided an extension of individual strength by helping each person do what he could not accomplish alone.

Anderson did not formulate specific answers to specific aspects of the problems that he probed during almost all his adult life, nor had he really expected to do so. Rather what he sought and eventually found was a code of values embracing his faith in intrinsic human worth. When this code was adopted by the government as well as by individuals, he believed that specific problems would be solved by action controlled by compassion for man, and he lived long enough to ensure himself that the ultimate solution to the specific problems was within reach as the New Deal extended its influence. While this social revolution would not remove the ultimate tragedy of human life, it would permit the individual to endure that tragedy with a measure of dignity that the old system had denied him.

This last period was not a time of frustration, of despair, and of degeneration of creative powers, as some critics maintain. Rather, it was a productive time; a time of optimism, and a time of fulfillment. His reputation among critics was still low, as it had been for more than ten years, but he knew that a reputation was mere appearance and as such, unimportant. Understanding of others was

the important thing, and he had devoted his life to it. Shortly before
his death he wrote, "If real understanding is to grow, it cannot be
done by politicians and businessmen. There must be, instead, a flow
of ideas back and forth, a flow of feeling." He was writing specifically
about his view of relations with other countries, but he was writing
too of his view of the relations among men. This was what he had
been striving for in his writing and in his life.

In the works of his last few years Anderson attained intellectual
maturity in his rejection of rebellion as a satisfactory solution to
social and economic evil; and he indicated in his handling of complex thematic material in *Kit Brandon* and "Brother Death" that he
maintained his hold on artistic craftsmanship. The final works, *Home
Town* and *Memoirs* reassert his stylistic powers; they provide final
affirmation of the human values he sought, and they remain effective
re-creations of a vanished society.

10

SHERWOOD ANDERSON
IN RETROSPECT

AFTER an active literary career of nearly 30 years, Sherwood Anderson was in critical disfavor when he died, disfavor that has persisted in spite of its paradoxical nature. Critical opinion has generally relegated Anderson to a minor position in American literary history, and yet it has not only been unable to ignore him but has continued to give him more attention than many figures considered to be major. The reason for this is obvious. When he was at his best, he was very good, so good, in fact, that *Winesburg, Ohio* and some of the shorter works have become modern classics. On the other hand, when he was being most determinedly modern and artistic, as in *Many Marriages* and most of the later novels, he imposed a kind of dating on his work that made it old-fashioned almost as soon as it was written.

Behind this dichotomy in his work lies another reason for the continuation of critical examination in spite of the absolute pronouncements made by critics. Even while he was still alive, Anderson had become somewhat of a mythical figure, who, perhaps more than any other American, embodied the dream of almost every critic, academic or commercial, who has ever approached him. The myth has maintained that almost alone among people prominent in the history of twentieth-century American literature, Anderson had the courage to reject commercial success and to devote himself to his art. That this does not correspond exactly to the facts of his life has been pointed out by numerous academic critics, but such disagreement is unimportant because the Anderson myth is apparently embedded as firmly as the George Washington-cherry tree legend in American folklore.

The dichotomy in Anderson's work and the myth that has grown up around his life have resulted in two emotional stances that dominate Anderson criticism: a harshness, which stems from the difficulty in reconciling the two extremes of his work; and a sentimentality, which results from personal identification with the problem behind the myth of his life. These two emotional approaches have become so commonplace that they sometimes exist side by side in the same critical study, resulting in a stereotyped approach that hinders evaluation of Anderson's work, understanding of what he was attempting to do, and recognition of the importance of the close relationship between his work and the American experience through which he lived.

Winesburg, Ohio and a number of individual short stories, notably "I Want to Know Why," "I'm a Fool," "The Egg," and "The Man Who Became a Woman," have been frequently and justifiably pointed out as Anderson's permanent contributions to American literature; *Poor White* is often added to the list. These works, however, are the products of Anderson's earlier active career, when he still received wide critical acceptance, and their worth has never been seriously questioned. At the same time the list ignores the fact that the short stories have been lifted out of the context of the volumes in which they appeared and have lost much of their meaning and effectiveness in the process. This generally acknowledged list is accurate as far as it goes, but it is incomplete. To these products of his early period must be added all of *The Triumph of the Egg* and *Horses and Men,* not only because they include such other excellent stories as "Seeds," "Unlighted Lamps," "The Sad Horn Blowers," and "An Ohio Pagan," but because they are collections of comparatively even quality. These collections are unified by both structure and theme to comment on the nature of men's lives as effectively and as perceptively as does *Winesburg, Ohio.* Stories and sketches are included that are less satisfactory than the best, just as there are in *Winesburg,* but to ignore the subtlety with which Anderson brought unity out of apparent diversity is to ignore one of his greatest skills.

Because too many critics suggest that Anderson had lost his effectiveness at this point, worthwhile contributions of his later periods are unfortunately ignored. To the list of his permanent contributions must be added parts of *A Story Teller's Story,* especially Book One and a number of other sections. This volume does contain the same old stuff, as many critics are quick to point out, and the book as a whole is uneven in execution. Yet both structurally and stylistically Anderson is often at his best in it, reproducing the Midwestern rhythms and idioms almost flawlessly and incorporating them in the old oral storytelling tradition, thus elevating that same old subject matter to the realm of American mythology.

From the last 12 years of Anderson's career it is necessary to add parts of *Beyond Desire,* the complete volumes *Death in the Woods* and *Kit Brandon,* the incomplete *Memoirs,* and numerous essays from *Hello Towns!, Puzzled America,* and other sources. The first is not only his most consistently high level collection of stories, but it also contains two of his best, "Death in the Woods" and "Brother Death." *Death in the Woods* is an integrated and mature examination of Anderson's belief that reality must be separated from appearance if truth is to be recognized and understood. The collection as a whole is as good as anything he had done in the earlier years.

Kit Brandon is his most objective and most fully realized novel, suffering only from carelessness and inattention, neither of which is sufficiently serious to condemn it. In this novel Anderson comes close to understanding the nature of the American experience as a product of the peculiar circumstances inherent in the growth of the country, an achievement matched in his own work only by the incomplete *Memoirs,* his attempt at a definitive interpretation of the American experience as he had known it.

The best of the essays are parts of this interpretation. Each of them is an attempt to come closer to an understanding of a moment in space and time, whether it concerned an individual, a group, or a set of circumstances. Each one of these better essays is dominated by careful attention to craftsmanship as well as by penetrating, intuitive understanding of the essence of the material; in them Anderson focuses attention on the significance of the small, the seemingly unimportant, and the easily ignored in human life.

All of these cited works must be included in a convenient list of Anderson's permanent contributions to American literature, a list that, while it is not imposing, is substantial and significant. But in order to understand Anderson and what he was trying to do, it is not enough to limit attention to any list of his most successful works. Rather, as this study has attempted to show, Anderson's work can be regarded only as a whole composed of many parts, because the major theme to which he devoted his attention was the meaning of the American experience as he had known and lived it.

Anderson's work in its entirety is an attempt to penetrate appearance and to determine the nature of the reality beneath it. To

Anderson, material manifestations were unimportant. He did not deny their existence; on the contrary, as in the case of the twisted apples left to rot in the orchards near Clyde, he knew that appearance was in some odd way often related to essential nature, but that the relationship was often ignored or misunderstood. This realization came early to him, certainly by the time he had established himself in business in Elyria. The literary career that followed resulted from the impact of that discovery on his mind—a mind essentially untrained and uneducated, a mind that found its way to a satisfactory resolution of the dilemma only through a long process of trial and error and of acceptance and rejection.

For Anderson the most obvious discrepancy between appearance and reality was the difference between the American ideal as he had learned it and its actuality as he had seen it put into practice during the years when America became dominated by material things at the cost of the values inherent in the ideal. The attempt to separate traditional values from a subverting materialistic ethic led him into literature by way of a back door because the words he had learned to use effectively in advertising were the only means he had by which to attack this distortion and confusion of values. In actuality Anderson began his literary career as a propagandist fighting against the corruption of the American ideal by materialism.

However, by the time he finished *Marching Men,* Anderson learned that there was no easy answer to the problem, and the discovery made him a writer instead of a propagandist. His goal had not changed, but he realized that the means by which he had sought to bring it to fruition were insufficient. Between 1915 and 1918 he began a tentative analysis that would lead him deeply into his subject matter, at the same time realizing the necessity of evolving a stylistic technique that would make his writing effective rather than merely functional.

With the writing of *Winesburg, Ohio* he had not forsaken his purpose to determine the relation between nature and experience and appearance and reality; he had merely intensified it by closely examining individuals who had been crippled spiritually by the confusion of values in a confused society. Encouraged by the success of his approach, he broadened it in following works, attempting to incorporate more of his experience into them. But he found that there still were no answers to his problem, a problem that became increasingly personal as he realized that he, too, had been confusing many things for a long time. Once again he shifted his direction and narrowed his scope in order to subject his experience to closer scrutiny. The introspection that followed enabled him to accept his inability to reconcile the apparent dichotomies in life, while penetration of his own life gave him a sense of identity and a sense of his role in life. These new insights pointed out the values that he had thus far been unable to define in his works.

Out of this crucial period Anderson formulated the concepts that dominated his later work and that remain as his final comments on the meaning of the American experience as it had been reflected in his own life. They were simple enough; so simple that they seem naive, even though their simplicity emphasizes their depth. The identity and the place he chose for his own were those he had misunderstood and rejected when he had accepted the appearance on which a material society is constructed. After re-establishing himself as an artist-craftsman who belonged in a town rather than to a center of materialism, he could go on to formulate his concepts of the nature of the reality behind experience. They were actually concepts that he had intuitively recognized when he first realized the existence of the discrepancy between appearance and reality, and they had been reflected in his work from the beginning. Through compassion and through empathetic understanding, man could break down the barriers that separated him from his fellows. In the process he would recognize the true values in human life, the understanding and love that, mutually achieved, would make life worth living.

This is the essence of Anderson's philosophy, a solution to the problems inherent in human experience that is both simple and complex. It was easy to say, as he had long known; but, he tentatively concluded, it was impossible to realize. Close as he was to naturalism and despair at this point, he finally acknowledged that the end itself was an ideal, and like all ideals, beyond the capabilities of human nature. Hence he reached the conclusion that the means rather than the end—life itself rather than an impossible perfection—was the only meaning man could know, but it was far from a petty or an ignoble meaning.

This is the concept that dominated both his life and works from 1929 to his death; man is his brother's keeper, he declared, whether or not he would acknowledge the fact. It was the realization of this truth that made human life meaningful, and its rejection, brought about by a preoccupation with things, had led to the inevitable dehumanization of American society. The American experience was therefore one that demanded a careful and continuous examination if one would find meaning inherent in it. Its nature, as he pointed out, had been such that from the beginning it demanded that man concern himself with the material appearance of life in spite of its great potential, and consequently only the individual himself could prevent the material from completely nullifying his own potential.

Anderson's works as a whole record his discovery of this truth, one that a more sophisticated man possessed of more education would have accepted as obvious and would then have promptly forgotten. However, Anderson, like his nineteenth-century predecessors Emerson, Thoreau, and Whitman, was not interested in discovering the physical laws that govern the universe; instead, he restricted his attention to the obvious problems of human life and tried to find a way to live with them. The entire range of his works from *Windy McPherson's Son* to *Memoirs* is the record of his attempt to make that possible by finding the meaning inherent in human experience as he had known it.

Anderson belongs properly in that main stream of American idealism which had its inception in the self-evident truths of natural rights, was nurtured in the transcendentalist realization that somewhere beyond physical appearance lay the ultimate truth of man's fate, and fell into confused disorder before the combined onslaught of Darwinism and economic determinism. The confusion endured in a world suddenly grown complex, but by the beginning of the twentieth century the disorder had been replaced by a counteroffensive determined to show the evils inherent in a world dominated by materialism. Anderson was temperamentally suited to become a member of this counteroffensive, and he was a member in spirit long before he became one in fact.

The literary movement and atmosphere with which he associated himself as a writer is clear indication of his membership in the idealistic counteroffensive. The keynote of the Chicago renaissance was liberation, and it was devoted to freeing the writer from confusion and from the concessions that idealism had made to genteelness. Liberation to Anderson meant honesty, and honesty meant that the major issues in American life could no longer be ignored. The movement had its superficial aspects, as Anderson learned; at times it seemed to be dominated by superficiality, but its core was a determination to right old wrongs at the same time that it established a new and honest American literary tradition.

Before Anderson joined the Chicago group, he had been primarily a propagandist, focusing on issues rather than people. His reaction to materialism was instinctive and direct, so that the early novels, *Windy McPherson's Son* and *Marching Men,* are based on protest and rejection while they are expressed in the diction and style of late nineteenth-century popular literature. But the literary movement of which the Chicago group was a part taught him that what he was writing was not literature, and it pointed out his new direction.

In the context of the new literary tradition of protest and rejection, Anderson's relationship to his major literary contemporaries is evident in both his attitudes and his techniques. Although he often gave credit to Gertrude Stein for having made him aware of the potential inherent in words and style, nevertheless his affinity to others is much closer. He moved out of Miss Stein's orbit of experimentation after the initial impetus that it gave him and into a circle that was largely Midwestern—so much so that in its view of its birthplace it has been compared to the Russians by D. H. Lawrence.

The two major Midwestern novelists with whom Anderson can best be compared are Theodore Dreiser and Sinclair Lewis, while among the poets his closest relationship is with Vachel Lindsay and Edgar Lee Masters. Anderson has much in common with all of them although, at the same time, there are major differences. Like Dreiser and Lewis, Anderson protested against an environment that made people less than human; however, he was aware of a special kinship with Dreiser. But the protests of all three took different directions. For Dreiser there was no way out of the deterministic environment that his people were caught in, while for Lewis, there was no need to wrestle with the imponderables as long as one could expose and at the same time secretly understand and sympathize with a society devoted to externals. Anderson could not accept the naturalistic helplessness of Dreiser's people even though the evidence overwhelmingly indicated that Dreiser was right, and Anderson's people exhibited the same symptoms. Nor could he be satisfied with the indictment of a system as was Lewis. Instead he sought in his own way to find permanent answers, even after he accepted the impossibility of finding those answers and had to settle for the meaning inherent in the search and in love and compassion for his people.

In spirit Anderson is close to the poets Masters and Lindsay. Not only is the basic structural pattern of Masters' *Spoon River Anthology* close to *Winesburg, Ohio,* but both works penetrate below surface appearance to reveal the essence of repressed humanity; an approach that became Anderson's most effective technique. Masters, however, is protesting against the system in the *Anthology;* in *Winesburg* and the other subsurface examinations, Anderson regrets the shortcomings inherent in human nature that prevent deep understanding.

The relationship between Lindsay and Anderson is closest of all because these two, more than any of the others, sought to go beyond protest and condemnation and to find new and enduring values upon which to build a humanized society. Both of them sought a faith that was essentially spiritual and idealistic, although Lindsay, especially in his early years, was primarily concerned with a faith firmly rooted in religion, while Anderson rejected such values in favor of a secular, although no less mystic, faith. Both of them moved beyond rejection and rebellion and into a final and positive affirmation.

In moving beyond rebellion Anderson became most clearly an idealist and a romantic. He believed firmly that a life based upon compassion, love, and understanding could be found somewhere; and he sought it in the past, and in the towns, where man could live communally and close to nature at the same time, finding strength and mutual fulfillment in the process of living.

This is the Sherwood Anderson who is little known and usually misunderstood, and this is the Anderson who did much misunderstanding himself. He was a seeker once he realized that there were no easy answers and put propaganda behind him. In his search for the almost perfect world (he rejected perfection because it is not human) he fused his work and his life, and in so doing moved across both literary and ideological lines so freely that he confused both his contemporaries and himself. Although he considered himself a "modern," he looked back in spirit to a romanticism that freed the individual from his environmental confines. As an artist he attempted to be advanced and experimental, but his most effective style grew out of an old oral tradition.

The confusion and misunderstanding inherent in these contradictions affected both Anderson and his contemporaries to the extent that the idealistic and romantic nature of his work passed almost unnoticed during his lifetime. Instead he was called a realist, a naturalist, a modern, a Freudian, and a Marxist, all of which he was not. To a great extent he must have accepted the titles because he did little or nothing to deny them, and the title of realist that he often applied to himself implies a close adherence to surface phenomena that is merely the point of departure for most of his work.

This misunderstanding has continued to the present. Generally Anderson is still grouped loosely with naturalism and occasionally to the post-World War I Decadents, especially Ezra Pound and T. S. Eliot. However, Anderson's links to these groups are tenuous at best. Not only did he go well beyond naturalism in his search for answers to problems that he saw as essentially spiritual rather than deterministic, but from the beginning of his literary career he rejected the decadence that eventually drove Eliot into the dogmatism of the past in religion and politics as well as literature and Pound into incomprehensibility and authoritarianism. The answers that Anderson sought were no less individual than mystic, and they resolved themselves into a compassion for people rather than theories or systems of any kind.

On the other hand Anderson's affinities to D. H. Lawrence and Ernest Hemingway are quite close. Like Lawrence, with whom Anderson identified himself in the twenties, Anderson was concerned with breaking down the artificial barriers isolating men so that mature and lasting love might become possible, and again like Lawrence, Anderson did not hesitate to use physical love as the outward manifestation of a deeper spiritual love. However, in spite of Anderson's reputation as a daring and shocking writer, he could never bring himself to treat the physical aspects of love with Lawrence's frankness.

The relationship between Anderson and Hemingway is even closer. Not only did Anderson's literary style inspire Hemingway and through Hemingway an entire generation of American writers, but also the thematic ties between them are quite close. Essentially both of them are idealistic romantics whose people, hurt spiritually by a hostile world, have embarked on a search for meaning in spite of the fact that apparently there is none. Eventually both of them point out in their works that the end of the search is not important; that what matters is the way in which the search is carried out. This is the position that Anderson approached as early as in *Horses and Men,* while Hemingway arrived there much later in *For Whom*

The Bell Tolls. For each it came after a period of flirtation with despair.

After Anderson's idealism had rid itself of anger and indignation when he began his search for permanent values through his association with the Chicago renaissance, his search for the values that he could adopt and affirm led him to focus on people, on the individual human lives that make up the generality "America" that had been celebrated by others such as Carl Sandburg. In so doing Anderson found himself in the difficult position of trying to find abstract principles through examination of individual human lives. That he was never able to find those principles not only emphasizes the difficulty of the task, but more importantly, it provides the most enduring of his works—those in which he penetrates for a brief but revealing moment into the heart of another human being.

The durable qualities of Anderson's work lie in the closeness and persistence with which he came to grips with his purpose, and they lie in the subject matter, the techniques, and the spirit that he combined to give form to his theme. The experience that he chose for treatment in his work is the record of America as it moved from idealistic youth into cynical and selfish maturity. The loss of innocence concurrent with the rise of industrialism has had no more effective and conscientious chronicler. Furthermore, the people with whom he is always concerned are people who, still possessed of that innocence, find themselves lost in a society that no longer values either it or them. Anderson's portrayal, as he brings them alive, is honest, compassionate, and effective.

The durability of the style that Anderson made his own in *Winesburg, Ohio* and gave freely to the mainstream of American literature is unquestioned. As long as the American idioms are spoken in the easy rhythms radiating from the Midwestern heartland, Anderson's style will be recognized, understood, and appreciated by the people who gave rise to it, no matter what the current critical preference may be. In style more than anywhere else, Anderson has come close to reproducing and interpreting a vital part of the American experience.

The spirit of Anderson's work is the spirit of life, and this, too, will endure. The wonder of human life, a compassionate regard for it, and a compelling sense of discovering significance in the commonplace permeate his works, giving rise to a lyric beauty even in despair. Love, compassion, sympathy, and understanding are the human virtues that raise man above his animal origins and prevent him from being a machine, Anderson points out, while his faith in those virtues dominates his work. Life is not only the great adventure for Anderson; in the final analysis it is the universal value.

In an age that denies the values Anderson believed in even more emphatically than did his own, Anderson's place among the journalists and the sensationalists is smaller than it should be; and because of his shortcomings as a literary artist it will probably remain small in the over-all range of literary history. However, as a man who approached life with reverence, who spoke of it with love, and who provided some of the most eloquent expressions of both in his time, his place is secure.

SELECTED BIBLIOGRAPHY

ANDERSON'S CHIEF WORKS

Windy McPherson's Son. London: John Lane, The Bodley Head, Ltd., 1916.

Marching Men. London: John Lane, The Bodley Head, Ltd., 1917.

Mid-American Chants. London: John Lane, The Bodley Head, Ltd., 1918.

Winesburg, Ohio. New York: B. W. Huebsch, Inc., 1919. (P)*

Poor White. New York: B. W. Huebsch, Inc., 1921.

The Triumph of the Egg. New York: B. W. Huebsch, Inc., 1921.

Windy McPherson's Son, rev. ed. New York: B. W. Huebsch, Inc., 1921.

Many Marriages. New York: B. W. Huebsch, Inc., 1923.

Horses and Men. New York: B. W. Huebsch, Inc., 1923.

A Story Teller's Story. New York: B. W. Huebsch, Inc., 1924. (P)*

Dark Laughter. New York: Liveright Publishing Corporation, 1925.

The Modern Writer. San Francisco: Gelber, Lilienthal, Inc., 1925.

Tar: A Midwest Childhood. New York: Liveright Publishing Corporation, 1926.

Sherwood Anderson's Notebook. New York: Liveright Publishing Corporation, 1926.

A New Testament. New York: Liveright Publishing Corporation, 1927.

Hello Towns! New York: Liveright Publishing Corporation, 1929.

Nearer the Grass Roots. San Francisco: The Westgate Press, 1929.

Alice and The Lost Novel. London: Elkin Mathews and Marrot, 1929.

The American County Fair. New York: Random House, Inc., 1930.

Perhaps Women. New York: Liveright Publishing Corporation, 1931.

Beyond Desire. New York: Liveright Publishing Corporation, 1932.

Death In the Woods. New York: Liveright Publishing Corporation, 1933.

No Swank. Philadelphia: The Centaur Press, 1934.

Puzzled America. New York: Charles Scribner's Sons, 1935.

Kit Brandon. New York: Charles Scribner's Sons, 1936.

Plays: Winesburg and Others. New York: Charles Scribner's Sons, 1937.

* (P) indicates works available in paperbound edition.

A Writer's Conception of Realism (lecture). Olivet, Michigan: Olivet College, 1939.

Home Town. New York: Alliance Book Corporation, 1940.

Sherwood Anderson's Memoirs. New York: Harcourt, Brace & World, Inc., 1942.

Letters of Sherwood Anderson, selected and edited with an Introduction and Notes by Howard Mumford Jones in association with Walter P. Rideout. Boston: Little, Brown & Company, 1953.

UNCOLLECTED
STORIES AND ESSAYS

"The Rabbit-Pen," *Harpers' Magazine,* CXXIX (July 1914), 207–210.

"Sister," *The Little Review,* II (December 1915), 3–4.

"Vibrant Life," *The Little Review,* III (March 1916), 10–11.

"When I Left Business for Literature," *Century,* CXIII (August, 1924), 489–496.

COLLECTED WORKS

The Sherwood Anderson Reader, edited, with an Introduction by Paul Rosenfeld. Boston: Houghton Mifflin Company, 1947.

The Portable Sherwood Anderson, edited, with an Introduction by Horace Gregory. New York: The Viking Press, Inc., 1949. (P)*

BIBLIOGRAPHY

Aldridge, John W. (ed.). *Critiques and Essays on Modern Fiction 1920–1951.* New York: The Ronald Press Company, 1952, pp. 572–574.

Gozzi, Raymond D. "A Bibliography of Sherwood Anderson's Contributions to Periodicals, 1914–1946," *Newberry Library Bulletin,* Second Series, No. 2 (December 1948).

Jessup, Mary E. "A Checklist of the Writings of Sherwood Anderson," *American Collector,* V (1928), 157–158.

Phillips, William L. "The First Printing of Sherwood Anderson's 'Winesburg, Ohio,' " *Studies in Bibliography,* IV (1951), 211–213.

Sheehy, Eugene P., and Kenneth A. Lohf, compilers. *Sherwood Anderson: A Bibliography.* Los Gatos, Calif.: Talisman Press, 1960.

CRITICAL AND INTERPRETATIVE STUDIES

FULL LENGTH

Burbank, Rex. *Sherwood Anderson.* New York: Twayne Publishers, Inc., 1964.

Chase, Cleveland B. *Sherwood Anderson*. New York: Robert M. McBride Company, Inc., 1927.

Fagin, Bryllion N. *The Phenomenon of Sherwood Anderson*. Baltimore: Johns Hopkins University Press, 1927.

Howe, Irving. *Sherwood Anderson*. New York: William Sloane Associates, 1951.

Schevill, James. *Sherwood Anderson, His Life and Works*. Denver: University of Denver Press, 1951.

SELECTED ARTICLES AND BOOK SECTIONS

Anderson, David D. *Critical Studies in American Literature*, Karachi, Pakistan: The University of Karachi, 1964.

————. "Emerging Awareness in Sherwood Anderson's "Tar,'" *Ohioana*, IV (Summer, 1961), 40–51.

————. "Sherwood Anderson after Twenty Years," *Midwest Quarterly*, III (Winter, 1962), 119–132,

————. "Sherwood Anderson's Idea of the Grotesque." *Ohioana*, VI (Spring, 1963), 12–13.

————. "Sherwood Anderson's Use of the Lincoln Theme," *The Lincoln Herald*, LXIV (Spring, 1962), 28–32.

Blankenship, Russell. *American Literature*. New York: Holt, Rinehart and Winston, Inc., 1939.

Brooks, Cleanth, and Robert Penn Warren. *Understanding Fiction*. New York: Appleton-Century-Crofts, 1943.

Cargill, Oscar. *Intellectual America*. New York: Crowell-Collier and Macmillan, Inc., 1941.

Duffey, Bernard. *The Chicago Renaissance in American Letters*. East Lansing: Michigan State College Press, 1954.

Fadiman, Clifton. "Sherwood Anderson: The Search for Salvation," *Nation*, CXXXV (November 9, 1932), 454–456.

Frank, Waldo. "'Winesburg, Ohio' after Twenty Years," *Story*, XIX (September-October, 1941), 29–33.

Geismar, Maxwell. "Sherwood Anderson: The Last of the Townsmen" in *The Last of the Provincials*. Boston: Houghton Mifflin, 1949.

Hicks, Granville. *The Great Tradition*. New York: Crowell-Collier and Macmillan, Inc., 1933.

Kazin, Alfred. *On Native Grounds*. New York: Reynal and Hitchcock, 1942.

Rosenfeld, Paul. *Port of New York*. New York: Harcourt, Brace & World, Inc., 1924.

Sherbo, Arthur. "I Want to Know Why and Brooks and Warren," *College English*, XV (March 1954), 350–351.

Trilling, Lionel. "Sherwood Anderson," *Kenyon Review*, III (Summer,

1942), 293–302 [the basis of his later essay in *The Liberal Imagination*, New York: Crowell-Collier and Macmillan, Inc., 1948.]

BIOGRAPHICAL ARTICLES

Anderson, Karl James. "My Brother, Sherwood Anderson," *Saturday Review of Literature*, XXXI (September 4, 1948), 6–7.

Daugherty, George H. "Anderson, Advertising Man," *Berkeley*, No. 1 (October 1944), 30–38.

Dell, Floyd. "How Sherwood Anderson Became an Author," *New York Herald-Tribune Books*, XVIII (April 12, 1942), 1–2.

UNPUBLISHED DISSERTATIONS

Anderson, David D. *Sherwood Anderson and the Meaning of the American Experience*. Michigan State University, 1960.

Phillips, William L. *Sherwood Anderson's Winesburg, Ohio*. University of Chicago, 1949.

Sutton, William A. *Sherwood Anderson: The Formative Years (1876–1913)*. The Ohio State University, 1943. [The definitive study of Anderson's early years.]

ANCILLARY WORK

Anderson, Margaret (ed.) *The Little Review Anthology*. New York: Hermitage House, Inc., 1953.

INDEX